Communications in Computer and Information Science 1370

More information about this series at http://www.springer.com/series/7899

Xiaoli Li · Min Wu · Zhenghua Chen ·
Le Zhang (Eds.)

Deep Learning for Human Activity Recognition

Second International Workshop, DL-HAR 2020
Held in Conjunction with IJCAI-PRICAI 2020
Kyoto, Japan, January 8, 2021
Proceedings

Springer

Editors
Xiaoli Li (iD)
Institute for Infocomm Research, A*STAR
Singapore, Singapore

Min Wu (iD)
Institute for Infocomm Research, A*STAR
Singapore, Singapore

Zhenghua Chen (iD)
Institute for Infocomm Research, A*STAR
Singapore, Singapore

Le Zhang (iD)
Institute for Infocomm Research, A*STAR
Singapore, Singapore

ISSN 1865-0929   ISSN 1865-0937   (electronic)
Communications in Computer and Information Science
ISBN 978-981-16-0574-1   ISBN 978-981-16-0575-8   (eBook)
https://doi.org/10.1007/978-981-16-0575-8

This Springer imprint is published by the registered company Springer Nature Singapore Pte Ltd.
The registered company address is: 152 Beach Road, #21-01/04 Gateway East, Singapore 189721, Singapore

Preface

1 Introduction

Human activity recognition (HAR) can benefit various applications, such as health-care services and smart home applications [1, 2, 10]. Owing to the rapid development of wireless sensor networks, a large amount of data can be collected for the recognition of human activities with different kinds of sensors [4]. Conventional machine learning algorithms require to manually extract representative features from data [3]. However, manual feature engineering requires expert knowledge and will inevitably miss implicit features. Recently, deep learning has achieved great success in many challenging research areas [5]. The biggest merit of deep learning is that it is able to automatically learn representative features from massive data. It can be a good candidate for human activity recognition [8, 9].

The 2nd International Workshop on Deep Learning for Human Activity Recognition, held in conjunction with IJCAI-PRICAI 2020, was intended to prompt state-of-the-art approaches on deep learning for human activity recognition. Ten research papers were accepted by this workshop. The details are shown in the following section.

1.1 Organization of the Chapters

Wearable sensors are widely used for human activity recognition, due to the properties of low cost and ease of use [6]. The first paper, *Human Activity Recognition using Wearable Sensors: Review, Challenges, Evaluation Benchmark*, by Abdel-Salam et al., first reviews top-performing techniques for human activity recognition. They use a standardized evaluation benchmark on these techniques via six public datasets. Finally, they propose a hybrid of enhanced handcrafted features and a neural network architecture, which achieves a superior performance over the state-of-the-arts on three datasets. The second paper, *Wheelchair Behavior Recognition for Visualizing Sidewalk Accessibility by Deep Neural Networks*, by Watanabe et al., presents a wheelchair behavior recognition system for visualizing sidewalk accessibility. First, they designed a supervised convolutional neural network for the classification of road surface condition based on acceleration data. Then, a weakly supervised method was adopted to extract features without labeled data. Finally, a self-supervised variational autoencoder was developed for classification. The third paper, *Toward Data Augmentation and Interpretation in Sensor-Based Fine-Grained Hand Activity Recognition*, by Luo et al., proposes a convolution-based Generative Adversarial Networks (GAN) approach for data augmentation on temporal data of acceleration, which is utilized for fine-grained hand activity recognition. The proposed GAN consists of a 2D-Convolution discriminator and a 2D-Transposed Convolution generator. Experimental results indicate that their method effectively improved the accuracy of the classifier with the augmented data. The fourth paper, *Personalization Models for Human Activity Recognition With*

Distribution Matching-Based Metrics, by Nguyen et al., proposes personalization models by using the nearest-FID-neighbors neighbors and FID-graph clustering techniques to group users with similar behaviors into the same community. They adopted the DeepConvLSTM model for training and testing with the data from the same community. The fifth paper, *Resource-Constrained Federated Learning with Heterogeneous Labels and Models for Human Activity Recognition*, by Gudur and Perepu, proposes a framework with two different versions for federated label-based aggregation, i.e., Model Distillation Update and Weighted α-update, when handling heterogeneities in labels (activities) across users for human activity recognition. Evaluation on the Heterogeneity Human Activity Recognition (HHAR) dataset indicates the feasibility of their proposed framework on devices for federated learning.

In addition to wearable sensor-based methods, vision-based activity recognition is also popular [7]. The first paper, *ARID: A New Dataset for Recognizing Action in the Dark*, by Xu et al., provides a new dataset, i.e., the Action Recognition in the Dark (ARID) dataset, considering the lack of available datasets for action recognition in dark videos. They benchmarked the performance of existing action recognition algorithms on this dataset and investigated potential solutions to enhance the performance. It turns out that existing methods may not be effective for action recognition in dark videos. The second paper, *Single Run Action Detector over Video Stream - A Privacy Preserving Approach*, by Saravanan et al., proposes a Single Run Action Detector (S-RAD) which is built upon Faster-RCNN combined with temporal shift modeling and segment-based sampling for capturing human actions. Evaluation results on UCF-Sports and UR Fall dataset indicate that their proposed method can achieve comparable performance with state-of-the-arts, but with significantly lower model size, computation demand and the ability of real-time execution on edge devices. The third paper, *Efficacy of Model Fine-Tuning for Personalized Dynamic Gesture Recognition*, by Guo et al., explores fine-tuning of personalized models from a global model for gesture recognition. They evaluated the impact of four different options on model performance, i.e., fine-tuning the earlier vs the later layers of the network, number of user-specific training samples, batch size, and learning rate. The results indicate that a proper selection of fine-tuning schemes and hyperparameters will boost the performance of the personalized models.

Finally, there are two papers that consider the adoption of Natural Language Processing (NLP) techniques for human behavior and activity recognition. The first paper, *Fully Convolutional Network Bootstrapped by Word Encoding and Embedding for Activity Recognition in Smart Homes*, by Bouchabou et al., proposes an end-to-end framework for daily activity recognition in smart homes by merging a time series classifier and NLP word encoding. Specifically, they applied frequency-based encoding with word embedding to enhance feature learning, which was able to encode domain knowledge, resulting in performance improvement for activity recognition. The second paper, *Towards User Friendly Medication Mapping Using Entity-Boosted Two-Tower Neural Network*, by Yuan et al., proposes a user medication inference system based on NLP techniques. Specifically, they formulated the problem as a ranking task which maps standard medication names (SMN) to descriptive medication phrases (DMP) by ordering the list of medications in the patient's prescription list obtained from pharmacies. Besides, they used the output of intermediate layers and performed medication clustering. Evaluation results indicate that their solution can achieve state-of-the-art performance.

The organizers would like to take this opportunity to thank all the authors for their valuable contributions to this workshop, and all of the reviewers, who provided constructive suggestions and thorough reviews during the paper selection process. The encouragement and support from Springer throughout the preparation of this issue are also greatly appreciated.

References

1. Chen, Z., Jiang, C., Xiang, S., Ding, J., Wu, M., Li, X.: Smartphone sensor-based human activity recognition using feature fusion and maximum full a posteriori. IEEE Transactions on Instrumentation and Measurement (2019)
2. Chen, Z., Zhang, L., Jiang, C., Cao, Z., Cui, W.: WiFi CSI based passive human activity recognition using attention based BLSTM. IEEE Transactions on Mobile Computing 18(11), 2714–2724 (2018)
3. Chen, Z., Zhu, Q., Soh, Y.C., Zhang, L.: Robust human activity recognition using smartphone sensors via CT-PCA and online SVM. IEEE Transactions on Industrial Informatics 13(6), 3070–3080 (2017)
4. Dang, L.M., Min, K., Wang, H., Piran, M.J., Lee, C.H., Moon, H.: Sensor-based and vision-based human activity recognition: A comprehensive survey. Pattern Recognition 108, 107561 (2020)
5. LeCun, Y., Bengio, Y., Hinton, G.: Deep learning. Nature 521(7553), 436–444 (2015)
6. Nweke, H.F., Teh, Y.W., Al-Garadi, M.A., Alo, U.R.: Deep learning algorithms for human activity recognition using mobile and wearable sensor networks: State of the art and research challenges. Expert Systems with Applications 105, 233–261 (2018)
7. Rigoll, G.: Recent progress in computer-vision-based human activity recognition and related areas. In: International Conference on Pattern Recognition and Information Processing. pp. 3–7. Springer (2019)
8. Wan, S., Qi, L., Xu, X., Tong, C., Gu, Z.: Deep learning models for real-time human activity recognition with smartphones. Mobile Networks and Applications 25(2), 743–755 (2020)
9. Yang, J., Nguyen, M.N., San, P.P., Li, X., Krishnaswamy, S.: Deep convolutional neural networks on multichannel time series for human activity recognition. In: IJCAI. vol. 15, pp. 3995–4001. Buenos Aires, Argentina (2015)
10. Zhu, Q., Chen, Z., Soh, Y.C.: A novel semisupervised deep learning method for human activity recognition. IEEE Transactions on Industrial Informatics 15(7), 3821–3830 (2018)

Organization

Workshop Chairs

Xiaoli Li   Nanyang Technological University/A*STAR, Singapore

Min Wu   A*STAR, Singapore

Zhenghua Chen   A*STAR, Singapore

Le Zhang   A*STAR, Singapore

Program Committee and Reviewers

Ming-Ming Cheng   Nankai University, P.R. China

Xi Peng   Sichuan University, P.R. China

Vincent Zheng   Advanced Digital Sciences Center, Singapore

Sinno Pan   Nanyang Technological University, Singapore

Joey Tianyi Zhou   A*STAR, Singapore

Zhang Wenyu   Cornell University, USA

Jinming Xu   Zhejiang University, P.R. China

Zou Han   University of California, Berkeley, USA

Lu Xiaoxuan   The University of Edinburgh, UK

Zenglin Shi   University of Amsterdam, Amsterdam

Peilin Zhao   Tencent AI Lab, P.R.C

Karl Surmacz   Zimmer Biomet, UK

Wu Keyu   A*STAR, Singapore

Cui Wei   A*STAR, Singapore

Contents

Human Activity Recognition Using Wearable Sensors: Review, Challenges, Evaluation Benchmark

Reem Abdel-Salam$^{(\boxtimes)}$ ⓘ, Rana Mostafa$^{(\boxtimes)}$ ⓘ, and Mayada Hadhood ⓘ

Department of Computer Engineering, Cairo University, Giza, Egypt
reem.abdelsalam13@gmail.com, ranamostafamohsen@gmail.com,
mayada.hadhoud@eng.cu.edu.eg

Abstract. Recognizing human activity plays a significant role in the advancements of human-interaction applications in healthcare, personal fitness, and smart devices. Many papers presented various techniques for human activity representation that resulted in distinguishable progress. In this study, we conduct an extensive literature review on recent, top-performing techniques in human activity recognition based on wearable sensors. Due to the lack of standardized evaluation and to assess and ensure a fair comparison between the state-of-the-art techniques, we applied a standardized evaluation benchmark on the state-of-the-art techniques using six publicly available data-sets: MHealth, USCHAD, UTD-MHAD, WISDM, WHARF, and OPPORTUNITY. Also, we propose an experimental, improved approach that is a hybrid of enhanced handcrafted features and a neural network architecture which outperformed top-performing techniques with the same standardized evaluation benchmark applied concerning MHealth, USCHAD, UTD-MHAD data-sets.

Keywords: Human Activity Recognition · Neural networks · Wearable sensor data

1 Introduction

Human Activity Recognition (HAR) is a challenging problem that targets to predict human gestures through computer interaction. It facilitates human lives through a various number of applications. There are two main approaches for human activity recognition: video images-based recognition and wearable sensors-based recognition. Recognizing human activity from video systems relies on the camera. Not only does this approach require expensive infrastructure installations for cameras, but it also poses some challenges due to background, lighting, and scaling conditions that would lead to difficulty in motion detection. As for the second approach, human activity detection based on wearable sensors such as barometers, accelerometers, gyro-meter, etc. transforms motion into

---

R. Abdel-Salam and R. Mostafa—Equal Contribution.

© Springer Nature Singapore Pte Ltd. 2021
X. Li et al. (Eds.): DL-HAR 2020, CCIS 1370, pp. 1–15, 2021.
https://doi.org/10.1007/978-981-16-0575-8_1

identified signals. It offers an alternative way to acquire motion without suffering from the same environmental constraints as in the video-based approach as well as offering privacy for its users. However, activity recognition based on this approach has some limitations regarding obtaining sufficient information about all pose movements in the human body that may affect the performance negatively. It is preferable in industrial applications to use more than one input sensor for recording human gestures more accurately and boosting performance.

The focus of this study is directed towards human activity techniques based on wearable sensors. Although there were remarkable improvements in this approach, it is difficult to assess the quality of work in this field due to the lack of standardized evaluation. Our work is reflected in the following contributions:

1. Extensive Literature review for recent, top-performing techniques in human activity based on sensor data.
2. Due to different evaluation methodologies, it is hard to achieve a fair comparison between recent techniques. Therefore, we applied a standardized evaluation benchmark on the recent works using six publicly available datasets with 3 different temporal windows techniques: Full-Non-Overlapping, Semi-Non-Overlapping, and Leave-One-Trial-Out.
3. Implementation, training, and re-evaluation of the recent literature work using the proposed standardized evaluation benchmark so all techniques follow the same experimental setup to ensure a fair comparison.
4. Proposal of an experimental, hybrid approach that combines enhanced feature extraction with neural networks, and evaluation using the proposed evaluation benchmark criteria, achieving a competitive accuracy.

The rest of the paper is organized as follows: in Sect. 2, data-sets used are demonstrated. In Sect. 3, an extensive literature review of human activity recognition using wearable sensors is discussed further in detail. In Sect. 4, our proposed hybrid approach is introduced. In Sect. 5, the experimental evaluation of human activity recognition for several top works is addressed. Conclusion and recommendations for future work are outlined in Sect. 6.

2   Data-Sets

Datasets in HAR consist of two main types: Vision-based datasets and Sensor-based datasets. Examples of Vision-based datasets are KTH [19] and Wieszmann [9]. The Sensor-based datasets involve four types: Object sensors, Body-Worn sensors, Hybrid sensors, and Ambient sensors. Vankastern Benchmark [14] and Ambient kitchen [18] are examples of datasets based on Object sensors, UCI-HAR and WISDM [8] are datasets for Body-worn sensors, Opportunity [8] is a dataset based on Hybrid sensors, and the AAL dataset [2] is for Ambient sensors. We will focus mainly on this study on wearable sensors data-sets. For human activity recognition based on wearable sensor data, there are several open-source data-sets available that offer diversity in categories such as the number of activities to be classified, the number of sensors used, and the sampling rate. In our study, we conduct our experiments on data-sets mentioned below:

1. MHealth [8]
2. USC-HAD [24]
3. UTD-MHAD [7]
4. WISDM [8]
5. WHARF [4]
6. OPPORTUNITY [8]

MHealth dataset was collected from 10 volunteers performing 12 physical activities such as standing, sitting and relaxing, lying down, walking, climbing stairs, etc. The readings were collected using three sensors: magnetometer, gyroscope, acceleration. The sensors were placed on the chest, right wrist, and left ankle. All the dataset activities are balanced except for the last activity. **USC-HAD** dataset consists of 12 daily life activities: walk forward, walk left, walk right, walk upstairs, walk downstairs, etc. Those activities were carried out by 14 volunteers. The readings were collected using MotionNode, which integrates a 3-axis accelerometer, a 3-axis gyroscope, and a 3-axis magnetometer. MotionNode sensor was placed on the volunteer's front right hip. The challenge in this dataset that the sensors may not align their readings due to their different sensors' placement. Each sensor responds differently to the human activity performed. **UTD-MHAD** dataset consists of 27 actions (controlled condition actions): swipe left, swipe right, wave, clap, throw, arms cross, basketball shoot, draw X, draw a circle (clockwise), draw circle (counter-clockwise), draw triangle, etc. These activities were carried out by 8 volunteers. The dataset was collected using a Microsoft Kinect sensor and a wearable inertial sensor in an indoor environment. The inertial sensor was worn on the volunteer's right wrist or the right thigh. **WISDM** dataset consists of 18 daily living activities classified into Non-hand-oriented activities, Hand-oriented activities, and Hand-oriented activities. The activities include walking, jogging, ascending and descending the stairs, sitting, standing, kicking a ball, etc. Those activities were carried out by 51 volunteers. The dataset was collected using the accelerometer and gyroscope data from both the smartphone placed on the right pants pocket of the volunteer and the smartwatch placed on the volunteer's dominant hand. **WHARF** dataset consists of 14 daily life activities classified into five categories: toileting, transferring, feeding, ability to use a telephone, and indoor transportation. Those activities - brush own teeth, comb own hair, get up from the bed, lie down on the bed, sit down on a chair, stand up from a chair, drink from a glass, eat with a fork and knife, eat with a spoon, pour water into a glass, use the telephone, climb the stairs, descend the stairs, and walk - were carried out by 17 volunteers. The dataset was collected using an ad hoc sensing device that contains an accelerometer, worn at the right wrist. **OPPORTUNITY** dataset consists of 21 daily life activities classified into two types locomotion and hand gesture. These activities were carried out by 12 volunteers. The activities include standing, opening the dishwasher, opening drawer1, opening drawer2, opening drawer3, sitting, closing the dishwasher, closing drawer1, closing drawer2, closing drawer3, walking, etc. The dataset was collected using 72 sensors of 10 modalities, integrated with the environment, in objects, and on the body. The sensors include 24 custom Bluetooth wireless accelerometers and gyroscopes, 2 Sun SPOTs and 2 InertiaCube3, the Ubisense localization system, and a custom-made magnetic field sensor. The five X-sense inertial measurement units are placed on a custom-made motion jacket, 12 Bluetooth 3-axis acceleration sensors on the limbs, and commercial Inerti-aCube3 inertial sensors located on each foot. OPPORTUNITY poses challenges since it is an unbalanced, multi-modal composite dataset.

2.1 Data-Set Preparation

Before feeding data to the model, raw data needs to be transformed into identi-fied samples. In this generation process, data split into equally-sized small win-dows - or another term temporal windows. Temporal windows are then divided into train and test data sets. Temporal windows may suffer from overlapping in part of the window that may lead to a non-bias evaluation. There are three techniques to generate temporal windows - as mentioned in [12] - for fair exper-imental evaluation:

1. Full-Non-Overlapping Window represents a generation technique to assure zero overlaps between temporal windows.
2. Semi-Non-Overlapping Window is an alternative approach to Full-Non-Over-lapping-Window for sample generation with a 50% overlap between every temporal window. This approach will generate a high number of samples, unlike the Full-Non-Over-lapping approach. However, it will result in biased results since the overlapping content may be seen in training and testing.
3. Leave-One-Trial-Out is a novel approach for sample generation as discussed in [12]. The trial represents a raw activity signal per single subject. It guar-antees a non-biased evaluation and sufficient sample number generation. In this generation technique, trials with the same raw signals are not duplicated in training and testing data sets.

Table 1 provides a checklist of temporal window generation techniques sup-ported in each of the six open-source data-sets discussed above. For the UTD-MAHD dataset, it has been separated into two partitions UTD-1 and UTD-2 based on sensor position. Based on supported temporal window variants of our data-sets, we conduct our experimental results.

3   Literature Review

HAR is concerned with the ability to understand human behavior. Various approaches to recognize activities have been addressed. The aim is to build a model that predicts the activity sequence based on sensors reading. A consider-able amount of literature has been published in human activity recognition based on wearable sensors over the past few years. The next sub-section will provide a comprehensive review related to different approaches for HAR classification.

Table 1. Checklist of Supported Temporal Window Generation Technique for datasets

Data-set	Full-Non-Overlapping Window	Semi-Non-Overlapping Window	Leave-One-Trial-Out
MHealth	✓	✓	✓
USCHAD	✓	✓	✓
UTD-1	✓	✓	✓
UTD-2	✓	✓	✓
WHARF	✓	✓	✓
WISDM	✓	✓	✓
OPPORTUNITY	✗	✓	✗

3.1 Hand Crafted Methods

In handcrafted methods, methodology usually starts with extracting important features from the dataset, then applying a classical machine learning technique instead of using deep learning to do both. **Kwapisz et al.** [15] worked on **WISDM** dataset, and extracted features per sensor reading. The authors analyzed three classifiers - Multi-Layer Perception, J48, and logistic regression - to determine the best classifier. MLP out-performed the rest of the classifiers and achieved **91.7%**. **Catal et al.** [6] proposed to use a voting classifier between J48, Logistic Regression, and Multi-Layer Perceptron with the same dataset and set of features as [15]. Confusion matrix, AUC, F-measure, and accuracy per each category in the data-set were used for evaluation. It can be inferred that the features introduced by [15]: Average-A, Standard Deviation-SD, Average Absolute Difference-AAD, Average Resultant Acceleration-ARA, are the best representative features for sensor-based HAR since they achieve almost the same accuracies compared to deep learning models.

3.2 CNN Based Methods

Ha and Choi [10] introduced 2 CNN models: CNN-pf and CNN-pff. CNN-pf represents CNN models with partial weight sharing in the first convolutional layer and full weight sharing in the second convolutional layer. Meanwhile, CNN-pff represents CNN models with partial and full weight sharing in the first convolutional layer, and full weight sharing in the second convolutional layer. The authors used the MHealth dataset using the Semi-Non-Overlapping window, and Leave-One-Subject-Out. The mean accuracy for **CNN-pf was 91.33%**, and **CNN-pff was 91.94%**. It can be inferred that CNN-pff achieves higher accuracy since they apply partial and full weight sharing. The first convolutional layer tends to capture high-end features that help in boosting the recognition. This approach uses 2D convolution, which has fewer model parameters than applying 1D convolution. **Panwar et al.** [17] involved five subjects (humans), especially three arm movements (activities). The authors applied three different pre-processing techniques. Each technique results in a different dataset that is used for training. Two architectures were introduced: the first architecture is for the first two types of pre-processing, and the second architecture is for the third technique. Three validation schemes used: 1) Cross-validation evaluation 2) Leave-One-Subject-Out, 3) Hybrid evaluation - out of 4 repetitions, training with 3 sets of data taken from each subject, and testing with the remaining one set from each subject. The best Accuracy 99.8% was reported by Synthetic data using Cross-Validation. In the paper, there was limited information about Synthetic data. Since it is a private dataset, there might be a likelihood that the model is overfitting. The approach was simple compared to other HAR CNN-based approaches, which indicate that the datasets used were not challenging enough. **Kasnesis et al.** [13] proposed Perception-Net. It consists of a Deep Convolutional Neural Network (CNN) that applies a late 2D convolution to multimodal time-series sensor data for efficient feature extraction. The datasets used to evaluate Perception-Net was **UCL and PAMAP2**. Both datasets were normalized. For the UCL dataset, the validation scheme was the Leave-3-Subject-Out approach; meanwhile, for PAMAP2, the Leave-One-Subject-Out validation scheme was used. Model achieved **97.25% and 88.56% accuracy** for **UCL and PAMAP2** datasets respectively. **Bevilacqua et al.** [3] proposed a CNN network for HAR classification. The author collected an Otago exercise program dataset composed of 16 activities, which is further divided into four categories. The dataset consists of 17 participants. The authors segmented the dataset into small overlapping windows corresponding to roughly 2 seconds of movements. The evaluation was based on the **F-Score and Confusion matrix for each category. Burns and Whyne** [5] proposed two different models: FCN (Fully Convolutional Network) and PTN (Personalized Feature Classifier). The datasets used for model evaluation were **WISDM, SPARS, MHealth**. A four-second sliding window was used for MHealth and SPAR, and a ten-second window was utilized for WISDM. The validation scheme used was a 5-fold cross-validation grouping folds by subject. PTN achieved best results on MHealth 99.9% ± 0.003, WISDM 91.3% ± 0.053, and SPAR 99.0% ± 0.017.

3.3 LSTM-CNN Methods

Lyu et al. [16] introduced an LSTM-CNN model for HAR classification, using **UCI-HAR, Mobile health** dataset with a privacy-preserving scheme for model evaluation. On the UCI-HAR dataset, it was segmented using a fixed sliding window of 2.56 sec and 50% overlap. For the MHealth dataset, it was segmented in fixed-width sliding windows - 128 readings/windows. The model achieved 95.56% and 98.44% on the MHealth dataset and UCI-HAR dataset respectively. The authors use local and dense properties from convolution and learn the temporal structure by storing information in LSTM units by placing a CNN layer above the LSTM layer. This approach achieves better recognition rates for datasets with a high sampling interval since it takes into consideration the activity changes over a time interval. **Xia et al.** [23] proposed an LSTM-CNN Model for HAR classification. This model extracts activity features and classifies them with a few model parameters. The authors used **UCI-HAR, WISDM, and OPPORTUNITY**

datsets with some pre-processing applied. Semi-Non-Overlapping-Window was used to segment the data collected by motion sensors. The validation scheme used was leave-some-subjects-out, depending on participants' number in each. The Evaluation metric was **F1 score**. The Model achieved **95.80% on UCI-HAR**, **95.75% on WISDM**, and **92.63% on OPPORTUNITY, Gesture recognition**. The approach used the Global Average Pooling layer, which reduces the number of parameters significantly, allows faster convergence of the model, and decreases over-fitting.

3.4   CNN-LSTM Methods

Sun et al. [20] proposed a CNN-LSTM-ELM network and used **OPPORTU-NITY data-set**. Pre-processing techniques are applied to overcome challenges in the OPPORTUNITY data-set. OPPORTUNITY data-set activities can be divided into Gesture and Locomotion. The authors used the Gesture category in the OPPORTUNITY data-set. **F1 and accuracy** were used as a performance measure for the model. Experiments were conducted on the CNN-LSTM-ELM network and CNN-LSTM Fully connected network. It was found out that the ELM classifier is generalizing better and faster than Fully connected. The CNN-LSTM-ELM model achieved **91.8% accuracy for gesture recognition**, while CNN-LSTM-Fully connected model achieved **89.7% accuracy for gesture recognition**. **Wang et al.** [21] proposed a 1D CNN-LSTM network to learn local features and model the time dependence between features. The model consists of 3 alternating 1D convolution layer and max pool followed by LSTM layer, fully connected layer, and batch normalization. The authors used **international standard Data Set, Smartphone-Based Recognition of Human Activities and Postural Transitions Data Set (HAPT)** [1, 22]. The HAPT data set contains twelve types of actions. These actions can be classified into 3 types: static, walking, and transitions between any two static movements. The authors experimented using different model CNN, LSTM, CNN-GRU, CNN Bi-LSTM, CNN-LSTM. The best performing model was the CNN-LSTM, which achieved **95.87%** accuracy on the dataset.

Based on the recent works' findings, we conclude that the CNN-LSTM and LSTM-CNN techniques achieve overall higher accuracy. We believe that is a result of using LSTM layers as they take into account the history of the signals, which may lead to better recognition. The drawbacks of using such techniques that they take more computational power and time for training. The advantage of using LSTM-CNN techniques for human activity recognition is that the LSTM captures time dependencies first. Then, the features are extracted based on the time dependencies using CNN. However, using CNN-LSTM techniques, the features are captured first, then considering the sequence of the features in time. This methodology may not align well with time dependencies; thus, it will make convergence harder with more computational power needed. It can be inferred that the recent works use a different experimental setup, each proposing its own evaluation benchmark. Some wearable data-sets are private, so it makes it hard to reproduce the results and conduct a fair comparison based on the work findings. Due to the absence of a unified evaluation criteria on all recent works, we applied a standardized evaluation benchmark to perform a fair, non-biased performance comparison. We compare between recent works concerning the standardized benchmark in Sect. 5.3.

4   Proposed Hybrid Approach

This section describes our proposed hybrid approach in detail. Our methodology is divided into two stages: enhanced feature extraction followed by Neural Network architecture.

4.1   Feature Extraction

Before feeding our data to our NN architecture, features were extracted from sampled data. We used 12 features - 4 of them were proposed by [15]. In summary, the features are Average-A, Standard Deviation-SD, Average Absolute Difference-AAD, Average Resultant Acceleration-ARA, Maximum, Minimum, Median, Skew, Kurtosis, Interquartile range, Area under the curve, and Square area under the curve. After the extraction of features, scale normalization, and Principal Component Analysis (PCA) [11] is further applied to the extracted features to remove redundant features - due to window overlapping - that helped in boosting accuracy.

4.2   NN Architecture

Our proposed architecture consists of three dense layers followed by softmax of activity categories' number in the dataset. Our architecture consists of a fully connected layer of size 128, followed by another fully connected layer of size 64 and then followed by 32 fully-connected layers. We used Adam as an optimizer with batch size 16 and Leaky-Relu as an activation.

The 12 Features are computed per each sample window in the dataset. Then, our lightweight neural network trains using the extracted features as input. The neural network learns the hidden features and optimizes its weights to reach a higher recognition accuracy than other classical approaches that use classical machine learning techniques.

Our proposed hybrid approach is stable and lightweight, compared with other techniques. It has demonstrated high competitive accuracy for HAR datasets as well as it can be easily deployed on resource-constrained hardware. Last but not least, it is found to be compatible with HAR datasets with no modifications needed.

5   Experimental Results

This section outlines our experiments and performance comparison between different approaches under the same evaluation criteria. We conducted several experiments with respect to our standardized evaluation benchmark. The evaluation metric is discussed in detail below.

5.1   Evaluation Metric

Recent approaches discussed in Sect. 3 are implemented[1], trained and re-evaluated alongside our hybrid approach to follow the same experimental setup using a standardized benchmark: 6 publicly available data-sets and 3 temporal window techniques described in Sect. 2.1. We conducted our experiments using Google colab with 1xTesla T4 GPU, 2496 CUDA cores, and 12 GB GDDR5 VRAM. In our study, mean accuracy is taken into account as an evaluation criterion for results.

5.2   Experimental Set-Up

We conducted three kinds of experiments based on the validation technique used:

K-Folds Validation Experiment. For the first experiment, top-performing approaches alongside our proposed approach are being evaluated via the K-Folds validation technique. We conduct our experiment using: MHealth, USCHAD, UTD-1, UTD-2, WHARF, and WISDM data-sets, concerning 3 generation techniques discussed earlier in Sect. 2.

Leave-One-Subject-Out Experiment. In this experiment, the same set-up is used as in the K-Folds experiment. The difference in this experiment is that the evaluation is conducted via the Leave-One-Subject-Out validation technique for the Semi-Non-Overlapping-Window sample generation technique only.

Hold-Out Validation Experiment. In this experiment, we investigated the effect of different hyper-parameters on our proposed approach via Hold-Out validation. Two variants of our proposed model were introduced: Proposed Approach V1 and Proposed Approach V2. Proposed Approach V1 training was set for 250 epochs; meanwhile, Proposed Approach V2 was set for 200 epochs. This experiment is divided into two separate trials:

1. The first is to compare the two variants of our proposed approach alongside other top-performing methods and evaluate accuracies using the OPPORTU-NITY data-set and Semi-Non-Overlapping-Window technique
2. The second is to report the accuracy of two variants of our proposed approach: Proposed Approach V1 and Proposed Approach V2 using: MHealth, USCHAD, UTD-1, UTD-2, WHARF, and WISDM data-sets, with respect to 3 temporal window sample generation techniques.

5.3   Results

In this section, we conduct experiments mentioned in Sect. 5.2 to evaluate recent state-of-the-art approaches, alongside with our proposed method. Top accuracies and second-top accuracies are highlighted with bold and underlined respectively.

---

[1] Recent works are implemented using the same architecture and hyper-parameters as mentioned in their papers and re-evaluated using proposed standardized benchmark.

Firstly, we discuss the results of the K-Folds Validation technique experiment. Mean accuracies using Semi-Non-Overlapping-Window and K-Folds Validation are reported in Table 2. It can be inferred that our approach ranked top accuracy in MHealth, USCHAD, UTD-1, and UTD-2 datasets. For the WHARF dataset, Lyu et al. [16] achieved top accuracy of 88.99%. Xia et al. [23] ranked top accuracy with a 1.3% accuracy difference relative to our approach in the WISDM dataset.

For Leave-One-Trial-Window and K-Folds Validation experiment demonstrated in Table 3, our technique ranked top accuracy in MHealth, USHCAD, UTD-1, UTD-2 datasets. Xia et al. [23] achieved top accuracy of 91.02% with a 5% increase in accuracy compared to our method for the WISDM dataset. Lyu et al. [16] obtained top accuracy in the WHARF dataset.

Referring to the Full-Non-Overlapping-Window reported in Table 4, our approach ranked top accuracy for MHealth, USCHAD, UTD-1, and UTD-2 datasets. For the WHARF and WISDM dataset, our approach ranks third-best accuracy.

Based on the results of experiments reported above for Tables 2, 3 and 4, it can be concluded that our proposed approach outperforms state-of-the-art techniques - both conventional and deep learning techniques - for MHealth, USCHAD, UTD-1, and UTD-2 datasets for 3 window generation techniques respectively. For WISDM and WHARF, our approach, in most of the trials, has ranked as one of the top three best accuracies. We believe that the reason behind the drop in our proposed approach's accuracy for WISDM and WHARF data-sets is the low sampling rate and that only one sensor was used for signal readings.

Table 5 reports the accuracies of various techniques alongside our approach using Semi Non-Overlapping-Window and Leave-One-Subject-Out. Based on results in Table 5, it is found out that our proposed approach out-performs state-of-the-art-methods, achieving top-ranked accuracy using MHealth, USC-AHD, UTD-1, UTD-2, and WISDM dataset. Referring to the WHARF dataset,

Table 2. Mean Accuracy using Semi-Non-Overlapping-Window and K-Folds Validation. (-) denotes that the approach is incompatible with the dataset and window technique used

Approach	MHealth	USCHAD	UTD-1	UTD-2	WHARF	WISDM
Bevilacqua et al. [3]	93.11	-	-	-	-	-
Catal et al.[6]	99.84	91.18	49.06	81.07	66.42	90.60
Burns and Whyne [5]	95.54	-	33.39	69.05	62.40	98.82
Ha and Choi [10]	84.77	-	22.67	61.67	68.95	81.81
Xia et al. [23]	99.96	-	56.41	84.62	87.45	**99.65**
Sun et al. [20] (Fully Connected)	-	-	-	-	-	-
Sun et al. [20] (ELM)	83.34	-	23.63	56.06	57.06	-
Kasnesis et al. [13]	12.45	39.48	6.85	15.82	-	-
Lyu et al. [16]	99.77	-	61.53	86.13	**88.99**	99.47
Panwar et al. [17]	09.00	13.84	05.22	51.59	-	-
Proposed Approach	**100**	**93.48**	**71.62**	**87.98**	80.39	98.35

Table 3. Mean Accuracy using Leave-One-Trial-Window and K-Folds Validation

Approach	MHealth	USCHAD	UTD-1	UTD-2	WHARF	WISDM
Bevilacqua et al. [3]	89.62	-	-	-	-	-
Catal et al. [6]	91.76	87.36	47.96	80.35	63.87	80.11
Burns and Whyne [5]	89.77	-	33.64	69.02	61.59	-
Ha and Choi [10]	76.66	-	21.46	63.87	64.68	76.42
Xia et al. [23]	87.89	90.94	53.97	82.44	83.47	**91.02**
Sun et al. [20]	77.69	-	24.30	-	-	-
Sun et al. [20] (ELM)	80.27	-	27.46	48.44	61.92	-
Kasnesis et al. [13]	14.33	40.61	6.39	18.13	-	-
Lyu et al. [16]	89.17	-	57.10	83.64	**85.07**	89.19
Panwar et al. [17]	09.02	13.85	05.24	50.00	-	-
Proposed Approach	**94.76**	**90.94**	**71.00**	**87.18**	77.20	86.18

Table 4. Mean Accuracy using Full-Non-Overlapping-Window and K-Folds Validation

Approach	MHealth	USCHAD	UTD-1	UTD-2	WHARF	WISDM
Bevilacqua et al. [3]	95.96	-	-	-	-	-
Catal et al. [6]	99.55	88.79	47.01	80.32	60.76	88.84
Burns and Whyne [5]	93.65	-	26.46	65.55	57.70	96.46
Ha and Choi [10]	79.85	-	18.92	57.94	61.70	77.07
Xia et al. [23]	99.70	91.55	45.99	79.76	78.49	**99.06**
Sun et al. [20] (Fully Connected)	78.77	-	22.70	39.87	44.43	-
Sun et al. [20] (ELM)	62.20	-	19.79	37.46	49.18	-
Kasnesis et al. [13]	9.52	31.74	6.46	16.70	-	-
Lyu et al. [16]	99.33	89.92	52.27	80.21	**83.29**	98.46
Panwar et al. [17]	08.99	13.50	05.27	48.04	-	-
Proposed Approach	**99.70**	**91.68**	**70.48**	**87.84**	76.02	97.50

Lyu et al. [16] ranked top accuracy relative to our model with an 11% accuracy difference.

Table 6 demonstrates mean accuracy results using the Hold-Out Validation technique on Opportunity Dataset (Semi-Non-Overlapping). We investigate the effect of hyper-tuning parameters. Compared with other approaches, Proposed Approach V1 that is trained with 250 epochs ranked second best with 86.24% accuracy with 0.4% accuracy difference relative to [3].

Tables 7, 8, 9 investigates the effect of training our model with different epochs: Proposed Approach V1 and V2 via Hold-out validation. The results are reported via MHealth, USCHAD, UTD-1, UTD-2, WHARF, and WISDM datasets for the three-generation techniques respectively. It can be concluded that there is an overall increase in the performance of the model compared with K-Folds validation results demonstrated in Tables 2, 3, and 4. We believe it is a consequence of using the hold-out validation technique, whereas the model could optimize its parameters over the entire training dataset.

In our experiments, we investigated the performance of our proposed approach not only in terms of recognition accuracy but also in terms of time complexity. We analyzed the time taken for our proposed approach - with respect to

Table 5. Mean Accuracy using Semi Non-Overlapping-Window and Leave-One-Subject-Out Validation

Approach	MHealth	USCHAD	UTD-1	UTD-2	WHARF	WISDM
Bevilacqua et al. [3]	85.00	-	-	-	-	-
Catal et al. [6]	95.87	74.62	31.98	73.67	49.69	73.86
Burns and Whyne [5]	91.78	-	30.33	64.96	49.87	-
Ha and Choi [10]	75.69	-	19.49	59.58	59.13	59.28
Xia et al. [23]	93.81	-	32.60	71.02	65.13	-
Sun et al. [20] (Fully Connected)	78.48	59.13	18.97	51.17	49.39	-
Sun et al. [20] (ELM)	81.57	-	19.37	50.90	50.52	-
Kasnesis et al. [13]	13.23	44.45	6.68	18.40	-	-
Lyu et al. [16]	92.05	-	36.73	74.77	**70.95**	-
Panwar et al. [17]	09.01	14.72	05.23	40.63	-	-
Proposed Approach	**96.35**	**74.71**	**50.82**	**81.37**	59.29	**77.91**

Table 6. Mean Accuracy using Opportunity with Semi-Non-Overlapping-Window and Hold-Out Validation

Approach	Opportunity
Bevilacqua et al. [3]	**86.68**
Catal et al. [6]	85.45
Burns and Whyne [5]	-
Ha and Choi [10]	-
Xia et al. [23]	-
Sun et al. [20] (Fully connected)	-
Sun et al. [20] (ELM)	83.21
Kasnesis et al. [13]	83.48
Lyu et al. [16]	-
Panwar et al. [17]	84.22
Proposed Approach V1	86.24
Proposed Approach V2	85.78

Table 7. Mean Accuracy using Semi-Non-Overlapping-Window and Hold-Out Validation

Dataset	Proposed Approach V1	Proposed Approach V2
MHealth	100	100
USCHAD	92.72	91.83
UTD-1	65.70	66.51
UTD-2	85.64	82.71
WHARF	74.24	74.47
WISDM	95.57	97.18

Table 8. Mean Accuracy using Leave-One-Trial-Out Window and Hold-Out Validation

Dataset	Proposed Approach V1	Proposed Approach V2
MHealth	100	99.76
USCHAD	92.13	91.58
UTD-1	68.51	65.22
UTD-2	83.51	84.84
WHARF	75.04	74.73
WISDM	97.50	96.05

Table 9. Mean Accuracy using Full-Non-Overlapping Window and Hold-Out Validation

Dataset	Proposed Approach V1	Proposed Approach V2
MHealth	100	100
USCHAD	89.72	90.38
UTD-1	62.13	61.83
UTD-2	82.84	82.35
WHARF	69.82	67.84
WISDM	95.45	94.73

the standardized benchmark above - to extract the handcrafted features mentioned in Sect. 4.1 per sample window. It was observed that the time taken in seconds to extract the features per sample varies ranging from 0.008(s) - 0.03(s). We believe that the MHealth takes longer to extract features due to its long temporal window size.

6   Conclusion

In this study, an extensive literature review on recent, top-performing approaches in human activity recognition based on wearable sensors is addressed. Due to the lack of non-standardized evaluation, recent approaches are implemented and re-evaluated using our standardized benchmark with three data sample generation techniques as discussed in Sect. 2.1 to follow the same experimental setup for a fair evaluation. Our experiments were conducted via six open-source datasets. A hybrid experimental approach is proposed for human activity recognition. Features are first extracted using our feature engineering and then followed by 3-layered neural network architecture. Our experimental results demonstrate that our proposed hybrid approach has a strong generalization ability with high recognition accuracy, out-performing all state-of-the-art techniques for MHealth, USCHAD, UTD-1, and UTD-2 datasets.

Future work should investigate the impact of low-sampling-rate and high activity number datasets such as WHARF and WISDM. More features should be added to our feature extraction approach, and further hyper-tune our neural network approach for higher recognition ability for human activity.

Acknowledgments. We would like to thank Jordao et al. [12] for sharing datasets: MHealth, USC-HAD, UTD-MHAD, WHARF, and WISDM that have been segmented by the temporal window generation techniques publicly to the community.

References

1. Abidine, B.M., Fergani, L., Fergani, B., Oussalah, M.: The joint use of sequence features combination and modified weighted SVM for improving daily activity recognition. Pattern Anal. Appl. **21**, 119–138 (2016)
2. Anguita, D., Ghio, A., Oneto, L., Parra, X., Reyes-Ortiz, J.L.: A public domain dataset for human activity recognition using smartphones. In: ESANN (2013)
3. Bevilacqua, A., MacDonald, K., Rangarej, A., Widjaya, V., Caulfield, B., Kechadi, T.: Human activity recognition with convolutional neural networks. In: Brefeld, U., et al. (eds.) ECML PKDD 2018. LNCS (LNAI), vol. 11053, pp. 541–552. Springer, Cham (2019). https://doi.org/10.1007/978-3-030-10997-4_33
4. Bruno, B., Mastrogiovanni, F., Sgorbissa, A.: Wearable inertial sensors: applications, challenges, and public test benches. IEEE Robot. Autom. Mag. **22**, 116–124 (2015). https://doi.org/10.1109/MRA.2015.2448279
5. Burns, D.M., Whyne, C.M.: Personalized activity recognition with deep triplet embeddings. arXiv abs/2001.05517 (2020)
6. Catal, C., Tufekci, S., Pirmit, E., Kocabag, G.: On the use of ensemble of classifiers for accelerometer-based activity recognition. Appl. Soft Comput. **37**, 1018–1022 (2015)
7. Chen, C., Jafari, R., Kehtarnavaz, N.: UTD-MHAD: a multimodal dataset for human action recognition utilizing a depth camera and a wearable inertial sensor. In: 2015 IEEE International Conference on Image Processing (ICIP), pp. 168–172 (2015)
8. Dua, D., Graff, C.: UCI machine learning repository (2017). http://archive.ics.uci.edu/ml
9. Gorelick, L., Blank, M., Shechtman, E., Irani, M., Basri, R.: Actions as space-time shapes. IEEE Trans. Pattern Anal. Mach. Intell. **29**, 2247–2253 (2007)
10. Ha, S., Choi, S.: Convolutional neural networks for human activity recognition using multiple accelerometer and gyroscope sensors. In: 2016 International Joint Conference on Neural Networks (IJCNN), pp. 381–388 (2016)
11. Jolliffe, I.T., Cadima, J.: Principal component analysis: a review and recent developments. Philos. Trans. R. Soc. A: Math. Phys. Eng. Sci. **374**(2065), 2015020 (2016)
12. Jordao, A., Nazare, A.C., Sena, J.S.: Human activity recognition based on wearable sensor data: a standardization of the state-of-the-art (2018)
13. Kasnesis, P., Patrikakis, C.Z., Venieris, I.S.: PerceptionNet: a deep convolutional neural network for late sensor fusion. In: Arai, K., Kapoor, S., Bhatia, R. (eds.) IntelliSys 2018. AISC, vol. 868, pp. 101–119. Springer, Cham (2019). https://doi.org/10.1007/978-3-030-01054-6_7
14. Kasteren, T.V., Englebienne, G., Kröse, B.: Human activity recognition from wireless sensor network data: benchmark and software (2011)

15. Kwapisz, J.R., Weiss, G.M., Moore, S.: Activity recognition using cell phone accelerometers. SIGKDD Explor. **12**, 74–82 (2011)
16. Lyu, L., He, X., Law, Y.W., Palaniswami, M.: Privacy-preserving collaborative deep learning with application to human activity recognition. In: CIKM 2017 (2017)
17. Panwar, M., et al.: CNN based approach for activity recognition using a wrist-worn accelerometer. In: 2017 39th Annual International Conference of the IEEE Engineering in Medicine and Biology Society (EMBC), pp. 2438–2441 (2017)
18. Saeed, A., Ozcelebi, T., Lukkien, J.: Multi-task self-supervised learning for human activity detection. Proc. ACM Interact. Mob. Wearable Ubiquit. Technol. **3**, 1–30 (2019)
19. Schüldt, C., Laptev, I., Caputo, B.: Recognizing human actions: a local SVM approach. In: Proceedings of the 17th International Conference on Pattern Recognition, ICPR 2004, vol. 3, pp. 32–36 (2004)
20. Sun, J., Fu, Y., Li, S., He, J., Xu, C., Tan, L.: Sequential human activity recognition based on deep convolutional network and extreme learning machine using wearable sensors. J. Sens. **2018**, 8580959:1–8580959:10 (2018)
21. Wang, H., et al.: Wearable sensor-based human activity recognition using hybrid deep learning techniques. Secur. Commun. Netw. **2020**, 1–12 (2020). https://doi.org/10.1155/2020/2132138
22. Weiss, G., Lockhart, J.W., Pulickal, T., McHugh, P.T., Ronan, I.H., Timko, J.L.: Actitracker: a smartphone-based activity recognition system for improving health and well-being. In: 2016 IEEE International Conference on Data Science and Advanced Analytics (DSAA), pp. 682–688 (2016)
23. Xia, K., Huang, J., Wang, H.: LSTM-CNN architecture for human activity recognition. IEEE Access **8**, 56855–56866 (2020)
24. Zhang, M., Sawchuk, A.A.: USC-HAD: a daily activity dataset for ubiquitous activity recognition using wearable sensors. In: UbiComp 2012 (2012)

Wheelchair Behavior Recognition for Visualizing Sidewalk Accessibility by Deep Neural Networks

Takumi Watanabe[1]([envelope]) [ORCID], Hiroki Takahashi[1], Goh Sato[1],
Yusuke Iwasawa[2], Yutaka Matsuo[2], and Ikuko Eguchi Yairi[1]

[1] Graduate School of Science and Engineering, Sophia University,
7-1 Kioi-cho, Chiyoda-ku, Tokyo 102-8554, Japan
watanabe@yairilab.net
[2] Graduate School of Technology Management for Innovation,
The University of Tokyo, 7-3-1 Hongo, Bunkyo-ku, Tokyo 113-8656, Japan

Abstract. This paper introduces our methodology to estimate sidewalk accessibilities from wheelchair behavior via a triaxial accelerometer in a smartphone installed under a wheelchair seat. Our method recognizes sidewalk accessibilities from environmental factors, e.g. gradient, curbs, and gaps, which influence wheelchair bodies and become a burden for people with mobility difficulties. This paper developed and evaluated a prototype system that visualizes sidewalk accessibility information by extracting knowledge from wheelchair acceleration using deep neural networks. Firstly, we created a supervised convolutional neural network model to classify road surface conditions using wheelchair acceleration data. Secondly, we applied a weakly supervised method to extract representations of road surface conditions without manual annotations. Finally, we developed a self-supervised variational autoencoder to assess sidewalk barriers for wheelchair users. The results show that the proposed method estimates sidewalk accessibilities from wheelchair accelerations and extracts knowledge of accessibilities by weakly supervised and self-supervised approaches.

Keywords: Sidewalk accessibility · Weakly supervised learning · Self-supervised learning · Convolutional neural network · Human activity recognition

1 Introduction

Providing accessibility information on sidewalks for people with mobility difficulties, such as older, mobility-impaired, and visually impaired people, is an important social issue. One solution to this issue using information and communication technology is to develop an accessibility map as a large geographic information system (GIS) to provide accessibility information (Laakso *et al.* 2011; Karimi *et al.* 2014). In the existing methods for gathering large-scale accessibility information, experts evaluate sidewalk accessibilities from their images (Ponsard and Snoeck 2006), or accessibility information is recruited from volunteers by crowdsourcing (Hara 2014). These methods depend on human labor and are impractical when collecting accessibility information in

© Springer Nature Singapore Pte Ltd. 2021
X. Li et al. (Eds.): DL-HAR 2020, CCIS 1370, pp. 16–29, 2021.
https://doi.org/10.1007/978-981-16-0575-8_2

a huge area. The recent expansion of intelligent gadgets, such as smartphones and smartwatches, familiarizes people with sensing their activities (Swan 2013). Focusing on the fact that the acceleration signals of wheelchairs are influenced by a road surface condition, we have been proposing a system that evaluates sidewalk accessibilities from wheelchair accelerometer using machine learning. Notably, a wheelchair body is influenced by road surface conditions, e.g., gradient, curbs, and gaps, which become a burden for people with mobility difficulties. Human activities measured by body-worn sensors are recognized by applying machine learning (Wang *et al.* 2019). The possibility of various machine learning methods is investigated for activity recognition using mobile sensors (Plötz *et al.* 2011). Aiming at improving the recognition performance, convolutional neural networks (CNN) (Yang *et al.* 2015), recurrent neural networks (Edel and Enrico 2016), and their hybrid model (Yao *et al.* 2017) are investigated.

In this paper, we introduce our methodology to estimate sidewalk accessibilities by recognizing road surface conditions from wheelchair acceleration signals. Our goal is to realize a system that provides services to visualize sidewalk accessibilities and navigate safely designed routes for users. We developed and evaluated a CNN model to classify road surface conditions, a weakly supervised model to extract highly representative knowledge from acceleration signals without human annotations, and a self-supervised autoencoder model to assess the degree of sidewalk barriers for wheelchair users and visualize accessibility information.

2   Sidewalk Accessibility Visualization

2.1   Proposed System

This section introduces our proposed system for providing accessibility information that is helpful for all pedestrians, especially people with difficulties with moving. Figure 1 shows an overview of the system. The wheelchair sensor signals are measured by a sensing application downloaded on the user's mobile device or installed in the wheelchair. The wheelchair acceleration database is created by measured signals and annotations. After training deep neural networks, knowledge of road conditions is extracted from the trained network. Then sidewalk accessibility information is accumulated as a sidewalk feature dataset and visualized as a navigation map.

The simplest type of accessibility visualization using human sensing is simple wheelchair trails (Mora *et al.* 2017). Wheelchair trails provide practical information for wheelchair users regarding wheelchair accessible roads and facilities. Although the information is useful, it is not sufficient for all wheelchair users. The trail approach indicates if someone could travel in a location, but wheelchair users may have different mobility and accessibility requirements. The physical abilities of wheelchair users are more diverse than generally imagined; some users are trained like Paralympic athletes, whereas others may damage their bodies with only a few vibrations. Critical information for wheelchair users includes the physical state of the road surface, such as the angle of a slope, the height of a curb, and the roughness of a road surface. This information about the physical state of the road surface helps all people with mobility difficulties as well as wheelchair users to make decisions about access/avoidance of a

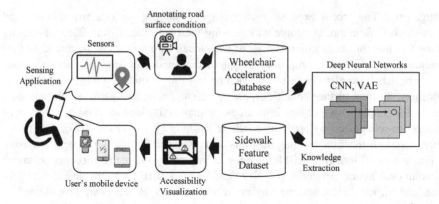

Fig. 1. Overview of the proposed system. Sidewalk accessibilities are visualized as a navigation map by using wheelchair sensor data and deep neural networks.

road according to their physical conditions and abilities. Therefore, the information about the physical state of the road is the foundation of road accessibility.

The vibrations of a wheelchair body are used for estimating the road accessibility information because wheelchair tires are directly influenced by the state of the road surface. Useful information is extracted from noisy raw signals of accelerometers installed in various wheelchairs because of the recent success of developing impersonal models by deep neural networks (Wang *et al.* 2019). Since extracting the only influence of road surface conditions from raw acceleration signals is challenging (Lara and Labrador 2012), the observed wheelchair acceleration signals must be converted into an index that represents the road surface condition. Our ultimate goal is to realize a system that provides road accessibility visualization services to every user by using impersonal models that improve its accuracy as new data is provided by users. As the wheelchair traveling data in more diverse places are gathered by more users after the service is launched, the model is incrementally strengthened. Along with the maturity of the model, it will also be possible to extract the road accessibility information from the running data of baby strollers and bicycles as from wheelchairs. This paper aims to establish a fundamental method of knowledge extraction from wheelchair behavior data using deep neural networks in supervised classification and weakly supervised or self-supervised representation learning.

2.2   Related Work

Various mobility support systems for people with mobility difficulties have been proposed. GIS applications are utilized to create a walking space network composed of information about width, step, gradient, and its location of the walking route (Yairi and Igi 2007; Zimmermann-Janschitz 2018). A navigation system for wheelchair users is provided on users' smartphones using on-site surveys (Koga *et al.* 2015). Although these mobility support systems are useful for impaired people, these systems depend on human labor, and collecting accessibility information in a huge area is impractical.

The quality of the road including depressions is detected based on a triaxial accelerometer and a gyroscope in android application using machine learning (Allouch *et al.* 2017). Abnormal traffic conditions in cities are detected using multimodal sensors of smartphones (Mohan *et al.* 2008; Yu *et al.* 2016). Although these methods evaluate road conditions using automatic processing, collecting detailed road surface conditions, such as gradient, curbs, and the roughness of a road surface, remains difficult. Therefore, we focused on developing a system to extract accessibility knowledge from wheelchair acceleration signals that can be automatically collected and are influenced by road surface conditions.

In the existing machine learning methods, a large dataset with teacher labels is required to learn road surface conditions from acceleration data. Manual annotation of the dataset depends on human labor, which is both expensive and impractical to collect extensively. The weakly supervised learning (Zhou 2018) method and the unsupervised feature learning (Längkvist *et al.* 2014) method have been applied to various machine learning tasks, including human activity recognition (Sargano *et al.* 2017), to avoid human annotations. This paper introduces our methodology to use weakly supervised and self-supervised approaches to extract accessibility knowledge by learning road surface conditions without human annotations from wheelchair acceleration signals.

3 Estimate Sidewalk Accessibilities

3.1 Dataset

The actual wheelchair driving data were collected to evaluate the proposed method. A total of nine wheelchair users between 20 and 60 years of age, including six manual wheelchairs and three electric wheelchairs, participated in the experiment. Their behaviors while driving about 1.4 km specified route (shown in Fig. 2) around Yotsuya station in Tokyo were measured by a triaxial accelerometer in the iPod touch installed under a wheelchair seat, and positional data were measured using the quasi-zenith satellite system (QZSS). Acceleration values of the x, y, and z axes of the accelerometer were sampled at 50 Hz, and a total of 1,341,602 samples (about 7.5 h) were collected. To confirm the circumstances when the acceleration data were measured, a video was recorded for both participants' driving state and the road surface conditions. Most of the entire route was a standard sidewalk, and a part of the course was a crosswalk. This route was carefully designed to include various road surface conditions to evaluate the generalization performance of the proposed method for common roads. If a user did not experience problems when moving up and down wheelchair ramp slopes, an excessive burden on the body and risk of an accident were considered minimal. Each participant drove the route in three laps; they drove clockwise from the start point to the goal point for the first and third laps and drove counterclockwise for the second lap. The slope and the gentle slope that were ascending clockwise in Fig. 2 were ascending for the first and third laps and descending for the second lap.

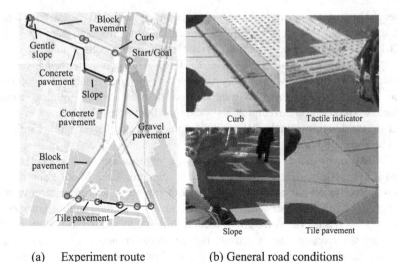

(a)   Experiment route   (b) General road conditions

Fig. 2. Wheelchair experiment route. (a) The experimental route driven by wheelchair users. (b) The general road conditions in the route.

A mean filter with a length of five was processed for the acceleration dataset to remove noises. Then, the acceleration dataset was normalized to have a zero mean and unit standard deviation in each axis. To input acceleration data to a CNN model, the acceleration data were segmented into 29,727 examples using a sliding window. The window size was fixed to 450 (about nine seconds) with 90% overlap. The window size and the overlap percentage were selected to be adapted for the dataset following the procedure (Iwasawa *et al.* 2016), which applied machine learning for wheelchair acceleration data.

3.2   Classifying Road Surface Conditions

This section provides a supervised CNN model to classify road surface conditions using wheelchair acceleration data. Road surface condition labels have four classes: moving on slopes (*Slope*), climbing on curbs (*Curb*), moving on tactile indicators (*TI*), and others (*Oths*). Each category represents typical road surface conditions: a continuous gradient, an abrupt step, a continued unevenness, and other conditions, respectively. These labels were created by visually observing the participants and the road surface conditions over the whole experiment video. The information on these road conditions directly conveys accessibility information to people with mobility difficulties, especially wheelchair users.

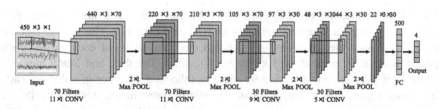

Fig. 3. The structure of the convolutional neural network to classify road surface conditions from wheelchair triaxial accelerations.

Model Architecture. Figure 3 shows the structure of CNN used to classify wheelchair acceleration data. The network is composed of an input layer, four convolution layers, one fully connected layer, and an output layer. The convolution layer consists of a convolution, a ReLU activation, and max-pooling processing. The fully connected layer consists of 500 units and a ReLU activation. The output layer is governed by a Softmax function that has four classes. The network has dropout layers after every convolution layer and fully connected layer. The dropout percentage is set to 20%, 30%, 30%, 40%, and 50% from the top to the bottom layer. This network follows the relevant research for recognizing human activity data (Yang *et al.* 2015; Takahashi *et al.* 2018), and the hyperparameters are adjusted for recognizing wheelchair accelerations. The Adam algorithm was used as an optimizer, and the learning rate was set to 0.0001. The test dataset was created by using a leave-one-subject-out (LOSO) methodology that verifies the performance for unknown users by evaluating a model with a dataset of a user who was not included in the training data. In this study, the model was trained repeatedly with a dataset of eight users as a training dataset, and the trained model was tested with the dataset of the remaining one user. The model score was evaluated by the mean of a total of nine trials. The validation dataset was created by dividing the training dataset into 90% training and 10% validation data using stratified splitting. The network was trained until the categorical cross-entropy loss of validation data stopped decreasing.

Classification Result. Table 1 compares the classification performance among the existing machine learning methods and the CNN model. Macro averaged F1 score (FS) and accuracy (Acc) were used as the evaluation index. Since *Oths* represented nearly 77% of the dataset, the classes are imbalanced, and the high F-score means that a model well recognizes barriers with few spots appearing in the dataset.

Table 1. Comparison between hand-crafted feature classification methods and CNN model in F-score (FS) and accuracy (Acc).

Method	FS	Acc (%)	FS	Acc (%)
	Without smoothing		With smoothing	
Raw + k-NN	28.2	75.5	26.4	74.9
MV + k-NN	45.0	69.9	45.6	73.2
Heuristic + SVM	51.9	80.3	51.8	80.7
Heuristic + MLP	56.5	78.2	56.3	78.9
CNN + SVM	62.6	82.5	67.4	85.2
CNN + MLP	**68.7**	**84.7**	**71.3**	**86.4**

The first comparison method (*Raw* + *k-NN*) used raw acceleration signals as a feature set and used a k-nearest neighbor (k-NN) as a classifier. The second method (*MV* + *k-NN*) used the mean and the standard deviation (MV) of each axis of each segment as a feature set and used k-NN as a classifier. The third and fourth methods used rich heuristic features as a feature set. The following 12 types of values of each axis of each segment were computed as heuristic features: mean; standard deviation; maximum; minimum; zero-crossing; mean, standard deviation, maximum, and minimum of the difference; FFT frequency component; energy and entropy of the FFT frequency component. The heuristic features were classified by SVM with rbf kernel (*Heuristic* + *SVM*) and multilayer perceptron with two 500 units fully connected layers (*Heuristic* + *MLP*). The parameter k of k-NN and the regularization parameter C and the kernel coefficient parameter γ of SVM were chosen using five-fold cross-validation to maximize the macro F-score. The parameter C of SVM and the loss function of MLP were adjusted to inversely proportionally weight to class frequencies in the training data to handle the class imbalance problem. To ensure the fairness of the comparison between these methods and CNN, the activation of trained CNN was classified by SVM (*CNN* + *SVM*) and MLP (*CNN* + *MLP*). Motivated by previous research (Cao *et al.* 2012), a smoothing method was implemented to post-process the predicted labels to enhance the prediction performance of the classifiers. Since the adjacent road surface conditions are in a similar state, the sample labels have a smooth trend. This smoothing method employs a low-pass filter to remove the impulse noise and maintain the edges. The impulse noise is a potential incorrect prediction, and the edges, in this case, are the transition in the road surface conditions. For the ith example, a smoothing filter with length seven was applied on the sequence whose center was the ith example. The predicted probabilities of the sequence were averaged for each class, and the class with the highest probability was assigned to the ith example.

The CNN method using raw wheelchair triaxial acceleration signals to classify road surface conditions achieved higher classification scores than the existing machine learning methods. This result shows that the proposed method is reasonable and practical to estimate road accessibilities.

3.3   Weakly Supervised Knowledge Extraction

3.3.1   Methodology

This section introduces our weakly supervised method to extract representations of road surface conditions (Watanabe *et al.* 2020). Our method uses positional information collected while driving as low-cost weak supervision to learn road surface conditions and does not depend on human annotations. The positional information can be automatically collected with acceleration signals and notably is semantically related to road surface conditions. In the task of weakly supervised feature learning, determining what information to use for supervision is an important factor that affects the learning performance. We attempted to use a novel method incorporating positional information during wheelchair driving as weak supervision. Since adjacent road surfaces have similar conditions, our model effectively learns road surface conditions by being trained to predict the measured position of the input acceleration data. For the positional information in this paper, we confirmed the position where the acceleration data were measured by visually observing the experiment video to correct errors included in the QZSS positional data.

Procedure to Generate Weak Supervision. As the first step, the earth's surface was divided into a mesh shape. The objectives of dividing the earth's surface are to aggregate adjacent road surfaces into one group and to create discrete classes to formulate the position prediction task as a classification problem. The width of each grid created by the mesh was selected to 5 m in both the vertical and horizontal dimensions because a grid width under 5 m can distinguish sidewalks on both sides of a road with two or more lanes. Then, only the grids that covered the driving route were used as target grids. Finally, a unique number was assigned to each grid of the target grids. These assigned numbers are the identification (ID) of each grid. These IDs were assigned to all acceleration samples. The grid to which each sample belongs was identified by its positional data. These assigned IDs are the positional label set and are used as weak supervision for acceleration data. Through these steps, the same class is assigned to the adjacent road surface, and the CNN model is considered to effectively learn feature representations of road surface conditions.

Position Prediction. The model architecture and the training procedure of weakly supervised CNN follow those of supervised CNN in Sect. 3.2, except that weakly supervised CNN used positional labels and the output classes were the IDs of the grids. We hereafter refer to this CNN model trained on the weakly supervised task as the PosNet model.

The result of the position prediction task of PosNet was compared to that using another machine learning method. The accuracy of the PosNet model was 11.2%. As a comparison of the proposed model, FFT frequency components of each axis of each example were calculated and classified by logistic regression. The regularization parameter C was chosen using five-fold cross-validation to maximize accuracy. The accuracy of the logistic regression was 5.86%. The pure chance was 0.32% in this case. The accuracy of these models is the mean of the total of nine trials obtained using the LOSO methodology. Although the score is low, the purpose of training the PosNet model with weak supervision was to learn feature representations of road surface conditions and accumulate them in the network. This absolute score is not important for evaluating the model.

3.3.2 Analysis

This section evaluates the representations of road surface conditions learned by the PosNet model. To evaluate the learned representations, the PosNet model was trained with the training dataset. Then the test dataset was input to the trained network, and the activation of the fully connected layer was obtained. This activation is a set of feature vectors and is the internal representation learned by the model from the input acceleration data. The obtained feature vector set was grouped by the k-means clustering to evaluate how well the learned representation conveys the road surface condition information. The clustering results were color-coded for each cluster and were plotted on the position of the input acceleration example on a map.

The route consisted of following 11 general road surface conditions: gravel pavement (GRAV), tile pavement (TILE), block pavement-1 (BLK-1), block pavement-2 (BLK-2), concrete pavement-1 (CONC-1), concrete pavement-2 (CONC-2), curb (CURB), ascending slope (ASC-SLP), descending slope (DESC-SLP), gentle ascending slope (GENT-ASC-SLP), and gentle descending slope (GENT-DESC-SLP). The clustering results were evaluated in detail by visually observing their plots for each lap. Figure 4 shows the visualization of the clustering result of one manual wheelchair user when the number of clusters k was 16. The ASC-SLP of both the first and third laps were clearly grouped into the purple cluster, and GENT-ASC-SLP in both the first and third laps were grouped into the light purple cluster. DESC-SLP and part of GENT-DESC-SLP for the second lap were grouped into the light green cluster. The most CURB were grouped into the yellow-green cluster on every lap. For other pavement types, GRAV and CONC-1 were grouped into the blue cluster for every lap, and most parts of CONC-2b were grouped into the green cluster for every lap. Although the clustering result of GRAV and CONC were similar for every lap, the clustering tendency of TILE, BLK-1, and BLK-2 were different depending on the driving direction. This overall clustering tendency was observed in all nine dataset patterns.

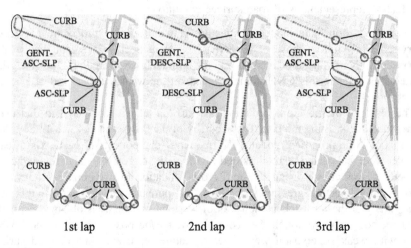

Fig. 4. The clustering visualization of the result of one manual wheelchair user. (Color figure online)

These observations demonstrate that the PosNet model learns feature representations of detailed road surface conditions. ASC-SLP and DESC-SLP were grouped into separate independent clusters, although the same position label was assigned to the adjacent road regardless of the driving direction. This result shows that the model effectively learned representations of the differences between the ascending and the descending gradient. ASC-SLP and GENT-ASC-SLP were grouped into separate clusters. This result shows that the model learned representations of slight differences in gradient. The exact points of most CURB were grouped into the same cluster for any lap. This result shows that the model learned representations of wheelchair driving patterns over curbs. As a summary of the clustering results of three laps, all 12 curb points were detected. The same pavement types were roughly grouped into the same cluster, and the different pavement tended to be grouped into different clusters.

The PosNet model was found to learn rich feature representations of road surface conditions through the clustering evaluation. The usefulness of the learned representation was evaluated for recognizing general road surface conditions. The classification task of road surface conditions was evaluated in a semi-supervised setting. A common scenario for a semi-supervised setting is that a large amount of data is available and only a small fraction is labeled. This scenario is realistically expected for wheelchair data because acceleration data and positional information of wheelchairs can be extensively collected, and manual annotation to all acceleration data is expensive and impractical. Since the positional information can be automatically collected, the PosNet model was trained with the entire dataset. Then a classifier was trained with a subset of road surface condition labels and their corresponding feature set, which was obtained from the trained PosNet model. *Heuristic + MLP* and *CNN + MLP* were selected for comparison to the proposed method (*PosNet + MLP*). In the case of *CNN + MLP*, CNN was trained only with the subset of the training data because the CNN model was trained with road surface condition labels.

Figure 5 shows the transition of the classification performance under the semi-supervised setting. The 100% subset is the extreme case of using the entire dataset. The proposed model (*PosNet + MLP*) exceeds the performance of the fully supervised method (*CNN + MLP*) when the amount of labeled data decreases below 10%. The performance gap between them increased as the amount of labeled data decreased. The proposed method (*PosNet + MLP*) always outperformed *Heuri + MLP* on any subset proportion. This result demonstrates the usefulness of the proposed method in a practical environment. When more extensive wheelchair driving data are collected than the experiment conducted in this paper, the performance of the proposed method improves even if the amount of labeled data is limited, providing a highly practical model.

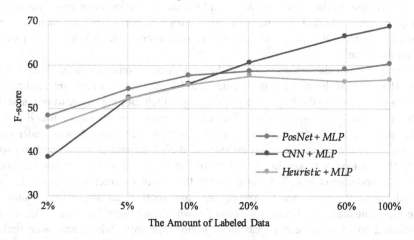

Fig. 5. The classification performance in a semi-supervised setting. The classification was implemented under 100%, 60%, 20%, 10%, 5%, and 2% subsets. The x-axis is logarithmic scale percentage of the amount of data with road surface condition labels. The y-axis is the macro F-score of the four classes.

3.4   Self-supervised Knowledge Extraction

3.4.1   Methodology

This section introduces our self-supervised method to assess the degree of sidewalk barriers for wheelchair users. This method attempts to use convolutional variational autoencoder (ConvVAE) to extract knowledge of sidewalk accessibilities from wheelchair acceleration signals. ConvVAE can detect anomalies even when no or small labeled training data is provided. The reconstruction error calculated by ConvVAE is examined whether it reflects the road conditions and is used as the degree of burdens for wheelchair users.

The ConvVAE network is composed of encoder and decoder. The encoder has an input layer, four convolution layers, and the decoder has four deconvolution layers and a linear output layer. The latent distribution of the encoder is sampled to latent representation that has standard distribution and is decoded to reconstruct input acceleration through the decoder. The convolution layer in the encoder consists of a convolution, a ReLU activation, and max-pooling processing, and the deconvolution layer in the decoder consists of a deconvolution, a ReLU activation, and up-sampling processing. The kernel size and the number of feature maps of convolution layers and training procedure follow those of supervised CNN in Sect. 3.2, and the mean square error was used as a loss function of ConvVAE. The window size in segmenting acceleration signals was fixed to 400 in this experiment so that the latent representation is reconstructed to the same shape of input. The reconstruction error was calculated using the mean square error between the input and output signals.

3.4.2   Analysis

The reconstruction error calculated by the proposed ConvVAE is plotted on the corresponding position on a map and examined whether it reflects the degree of burdens for wheelchair users. After training the ConvVAE model by training dataset, the test dataset was input to the trained network, and the reconstruction error was obtained for each nine users by LOSO. The reconstruction error was normalized for each user and the maximum reconstruction error value over nine users were selected within every 5 m on the route.

Figure 6 shows the visualization of the maximum reconstruction error over nine users. The color of the plot points is determined by the ratio of each selected reconstruction error value to the largest value. The larger the ratio, the closer to red, and the smaller the ratio, the closer to blue. The large reconstruction errors are found at five CURB points and Unusual spot-A in the figure. Since the spot-A was under construction when the experiment was conducted, the participant drove around the spot differently from other roads. In most parts of the route, the values of reconstruction error were moderate or low. This result shows that the reconstruction error reflects the unusualness of the road such as abrupt steps and spots in an unusual environment. Since these unusual spots become burdens for wheelchair users, the ConvVAE model is indicated to extract some accessibility knowledge from wheelchair acceleration signals without any supervision.

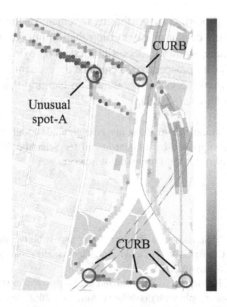

Fig. 6. The reconstruction error plot over nine participants. (Color figure online)

4 Conclusion

The contributions of this paper were to confirm the possibility of using wheelchair acceleration signals to provide accessibility information. This paper developed and proposed a prototype system for visualizing sidewalk accessibility information that helps pedestrians, especially people with mobility difficulties. The proposed methodology used deep neural networks to estimate sidewalk accessibility by extracting knowledge from wheelchair behavior via a triaxial accelerometer in a smartphone installed under a wheelchair seat. The supervised method demonstrated that CNN classifies road surface conditions by recognizing wheelchair behavior from acceleration signals. A novel method was proposed to estimate road surface conditions without manual annotation by applying weakly supervised learning. The proposed method demonstrated that positional information during wheelchair driving helps with learning rich representations of road surface conditions, and the learned representations were highly discriminative for a road surface classification task. The learned representations were visualized on a map and demonstrated to provide detailed representations of road surface conditions, such as the difference of ascending and descending of a slope, the angle of slopes, the exact locations of curbs, and the slight differences of similar pavements. The learned representations were found to be more useful than calculated rich heuristic features for the road surface classification task. The self-supervised section introduced a method to assess the degree of sidewalk barriers for wheelchair users. The proposed method attempted to use ConvVAE to extract knowledge of sidewalk accessibilities from wheelchair acceleration signals. The result indicated to extract accessibility knowledge, such as abrupt steps and a spot in an unusual environment that leads to a barrier for wheelchair users, without any supervision.

Our future work will be directed to the improvement of the wheelchair behavior recognition model and the design of supervision that do not require human labor and are beneficial to estimate sidewalk accessibilities. Employing recent hybrid deep models (Yao et al. 2017) are prospective to enhance the recognition model. The design of supervision includes unsupervised representation learning that could be employed for activity recognition (Ji et al. 2019).

Acknowledgments. We would like to show our best gratitude to all participants in data collection. This research was supported by a Grant-in-Aid for Scientific Research (B), 17H01946 and 20H04476, Japan Society for the Promotion of Science.

References

Laakso, M., Sarjakoski, T., Sarjakoski, L.T.: Improving accessibility information in pedestrian maps and databases. Cartogr. Int. J. Geogr. Inf. Geovisualization **46**(2), 101–108 (2011). https://doi.org/10.3138/carto.46.2.101

Karimi, H.A., Zhang, L., Benner, J.G.: Personalized accessibility map (PAM): a novel assisted wayfinding approach for people with disabilities. Ann. GIS **20**(2), 99–108 (2014). https://doi.org/10.1080/19475683.2014.904438

Ponsard, C., Snoeck, V.: Objective accessibility assessment of public infrastructures. In: Miesenberger, K., Klaus, J., Zagler, W.L., Karshmer, A.I. (eds.) ICCHP 2006. LNCS, vol. 4061, pp. 314–321. Springer, Heidelberg (2006). https://doi.org/10.1007/11788713_47

Hara, K.: Scalable methods to collect and visualize sidewalk accessibility data for people with mobility impairments. In: UIST, pp. 1–4 (2014). https://doi.org/10.1145/2658779.2661163

Swan, M.: The quantified self: fundamental disruption in big data science and biological discovery. Big Data **1**(2), 85–99 (2013). https://doi.org/10.1089/big.2012.0002

Wang, J., Chen, Y., Hao, S., Peng, X., Hu, L.: Deep learning for sensor-based activity recognition: a survey. Pattern Recogn. Lett. **119**, 3–11 (2019). https://doi.org/10.1016/j.patrec.2018.02.010

Plötz, T., Hammerla, N.Y., Olivier, P.L.: Feature learning for activity recognition in ubiquitous computing. In: IJCAI, pp. 1729–1734 (2011). https://doi.org/10.5591/978-1-57735-516-8/IJCAI11-290

Yang, J., Nguyen, M.N., San, P.P., Li, X., Krishnaswamy, S.: Deep convolutional neural networks on multichannel time series for human activity recognition. In: IJCAI, pp. 25–31 (2015)

Edel, M., Köppe, E.: Binarized-BLSTM-RNN based human activity recognition. In: IPIN, pp. 1–7 (2016). https://doi.org/10.1109/IPIN.2016.7743581

Yao, S., Hu, S., Zhao, Y., Zhang, A., Abdelzaher, T.: Deepsense: a unified deep learning framework for time-series mobile sensing data processing. In: WWW, pp. 351–360 (2017). https://doi.org/10.1145/3038912.3052577

Mora, H., Gilart-Iglesias, V., Pérez-del Hoyo, R., Andújar-Montoya, M.D.: A comprehensive system for monitoring urban accessibility in smart cities. Sensors **17**(8), 1834 (2017). https://doi.org/10.3390/s17081834

Lara, O.D., Labrador, M.A.: A survey on human activity recognition using wearable sensors. IEEE Commun. Surv. Tutor. **15**(3), 1192–1209 (2012). https://doi.org/10.1109/SURV.2012.110112.00192

Yairi, E.I., Igi, S.: Research on ubiquitous system for mobility support of the elderly and disabled and its technology transfer to industry. J. Inf. Process. **48**, 770–779 (2007). (in Japanese)

Zimmermann-Janschitz, S.: Geographic information systems in the context of disabilities. J. Access. Des. All **8**(2), 161–192 (2018). https://doi.org/10.17411/jacces.v8i2.171

Koga, M., Izumi, S., Matsubara, S., Morishita, K., Yoshioka, D.: Development and verification of navigation system to support wheelchair user activity in urban areas. IADIS Int. J. WWW/Internet **13**(1), 43–56 (2015)

Allouch, A., Koubâa, A., Abbes, T., Ammar, A.: Roadsense: smartphone application to estimate road conditions using accelerometer and gyroscope. IEEE Sens. J. **17**(13), 4231–4238 (2017). https://doi.org/10.1109/JSEN.2017.2702739

Mohan, P., Padmanabhan, V.N., Ramjee, R.: Nericell: rich monitoring of road and traffic conditions using mobile smartphones. In: SENSYS, pp. 323–336 (2008). https://doi.org/10.1145/1460412.1460444

Yu, J., et al.: Senspeed: sensing driving conditions to estimate vehicle speed in urban environments. IEEE Trans. Mob. Comput **15**(1), 202–216 (2016). https://doi.org/10.1109/TMC.2015.2411270

Zhou, Z.-H.: A brief introduction to weakly supervised learning. Natl. Sci. Rev. **5**(1), 44–53 (2018). https://doi.org/10.1093/nsr/nwx106

Längkvist, M., Karlsson, L., Loutfi, A.: A review of unsupervised feature learning and deep learning for time-series modeling. Pattern Recogn. Lett. **42**, 11–24 (2014). https://doi.org/10.1016/j.patrec.2014.01.008

Sargano, A.B., Angelov, P., Habib, Z.: A comprehensive review on handcrafted and learning-based action representation approaches for human activity recognition. Appl. Sci. **7**(1), 110 (2017). https://doi.org/10.3390/app7010110

Iwasawa, Y., Yairi, I.E., Matsuo, Y.: Combining human action sensing of wheelchair users and machine learning for autonomous accessibility data collection. IEICE Trans. Inf. Syst. **99**(4), 115–124 (2016). https://doi.org/10.1587/transinf.2015EDP7278

Takahashi, H., Nagamine, K., Iwasawa, Y., Matsuo, Y., Yairi, I.E.: Quantification of road condition from wheelchair sensing data using deep convolutional neural network. IEICE Trans. Inf. Syst. **101**(6), 2502–2505 (2018). https://doi.org/10.14923/transinfj.2017jdp7067. (in Japanese)

Cao, H., Nguyen, M.N., Phua, C., Krishnaswamy, S., Li, X.-L.: An integrated framework for human activity classification. In: UbiComp, pp. 331–340 (2012). https://doi.org/10.1145/2370216.2370334

Watanabe, T., Takahashi, H., Iwasawa, Y., Matsuo, Y., Yairi, I.E.: Weakly supervised learning for evaluating road surface condition from wheelchair driving data. Information **11**(1), 2 (2020). https://doi.org/10.3390/info11010002

Ji, X., Henriques, J.F., Vedaldi, A.: Invariant information clustering for unsupervised image classification and segmentation. In: ICCV, pp. 9865–9874 (2019). https://doi.org/10.1109/ICCV.2019.00996

Toward Data Augmentation and Interpretation in Sensor-Based Fine-Grained Hand Activity Recognition

Jinqi Luo[1(✉)], Xiang Li[2], and Rabih Younes[3]

[1] Nanyang Technological University, Singapore, Singapore
luoj0021@ntu.edu.sg
[2] Huazhong University of Science and Technology, Wuhan, China
xiangli_ee@hust.edu.cn
[3] Duke University, Durham, USA
rabih.younes@duke.edu

Abstract. Recognizing fine-grained hand activities has widely attracted the research community's attention in recent years. However, rather than enriched sen-sor-based datasets of whole-body activities, there are limited data available for acceler-ator-based fine-grained hand activities. In this paper, we propose a purely convolution-based Generative Adversarial Networks (GAN) approach for data augmentation on accelerator-based temporal data of fine-grained hand activities. The approach consists of 2D-Convolution discriminator and 2D-Transposed-Convolution generator that are shown capable of learning the distribution of re-shaped sensor-based data and generating synthetic instances that well reserve the cross-axis co-relation. We evaluate the usability of synthetic data by expanding existing datasets and improving the state-of-the-art classifier's test accuracy. The in-nature unreadable sensor-based data is interpreted by introducing visualization methods including axis-wise heatmap and model-oriented decision explanation. The experiments show that our approach can effectively improve the classifier's test accuracy by GAN-based data augmentation while well preserving the authenticity of synthetic data.

Keywords: Activity recognition · Data augmentation · GAN · Deep learning

1 Introduction

Recent years have witnessed the increasing popularity of Human Activity Recognition (HAR). Since deep learning has shown a strong ability to extract high-level feature representations from large data distribution, exploring such deep approaches for sensor-based HAR tasks is prospering around the research community [7,26]. In the recent decade, deep learning techniques have significantly optimized HAR tasks with a handful of human-oriented applications [20,28].

© Springer Nature Singapore Pte Ltd. 2021
X. Li et al. (Eds.): DL-HAR 2020, CCIS 1370, pp. 30–42, 2021.
https://doi.org/10.1007/978-981-16-0575-8_3

However, modern HAR research often ignores to recognize fine-grained *hand actions* from sensor-based signals since these hand activities are often independent of body activity. For example, a person can be recognized as peacefully sitting in a chair (body activity) while playing video games (hand activity). Such gaps make it hard to distinguish the hand action using sensors on other parts of the human body. Sensing fine-grained hand activity independent from body motions can inspire further development on context-awareness devices of health monitoring and assist in interactive game design. Yet, a very limited number of works have attempted to build deep-learning-based prototypes in this direction [9,17]. Therefore, it is still of significant potential to explore sensor-based hand activity recognition with various deep learning techniques toward building a more comprehensive and context-sensitive HAR system.

Despite the great success of deep learning, modern deep-learning-based HAR approaches are encountering significant challenges on data scarcity. In the context of sensor-based hand activity recognition, it is still an undeveloped area when it comes to solving the data scarcity problem when training deep classifiers for fine-grained signals of hand activity. Since hand motion data collection involves human labor and sensor purchasing, the collection process for such sensor-based signals is increasingly demanding with respect to time and money. The problem of inaccurate activity measurements also impact the data and results [25]. Furthermore, recently, the COVID-19 pandemic has made it very difficult to collect data on human subjects, especially for hand activities that are fine-grained enough for laboratory standard. Under these circumstances, data augmentation by real-world collection is difficult and sometimes even infeasible.

In the aim to bridge the aforementioned research gaps, in this paper, we propose a GAN-based approach to enable data augmentation of sensor-based hand activity recognition tasks, which improves test accuracy for training state-of-the-art hand activity classifiers. Our approach well captures the intrinsic correlations between time-series data of three axes in an accelerometer by adopting two-dimension Convolution Layers. Such approach also better learns multi-scale features in a single slice of time-series data sample. We train the generation models on real sensor-based data of 12 separate categories of fine-grained hand activities and then generate augmented datasets. After that, we re-train the state-of-the-art hand activity recognition classifiers with the help of our augmented datasets and evaluate the improvements on categorical accuracy. To further assess the synthetic data, we propose two visual inspection methods to evaluate the quality of the synthetic data and interpret the decision of hand activity recognition classifiers.

2   Related Works

2.1   Human Activity Recognition

Traditional non-deep-learning approaches mainly focus on utilizing techniques of feature extraction, such as time-series signal transformation [13] and hand-crafted statistical modeling [5]. Effectively capturing distinguishable feature representations has therefore been a major challenge in HAR tasks for a long time. Leading deep-learning-based HAR works have demonstrated the usefulness of deep neural networks in HAR [16,28]. Beyond that, some research tries to introduce ensemble classifiers or multimodal solutions that merge different channels of sensor data to improve the model training process of some challenging HAR tasks [14,20]. Following the deep learning trend, HAR begins to release its potential in many industrial and real-world applications, such as heart indicator evaluation [4] and accident detection [18].

More specifically, in hand activity recognition, some apply computer vision approaches to recognize hand postures and motions [9,21]. [17] introduce recognizing specific hand activities by sensor-based data from smartwatches, which is shown to be an underutilized yet a highly complementary contextual channel for HAR. Such recognition can have wide use in human-oriented applications like assisting in the translation of sign languages [24].

More recent HAR works are thoroughly optimized to learn latent representation of signals and make accurate classification upon that. Nevertheless, there gradually emerges the problem of annotation scarcity [7] since the data collection process in HAR is often noise-rich, expensive, and time-consuming. Some works proposed unsupervised or semi-supervised [6,12] learning towards solving this problem of data scarcity, but few have adopted the concept of Generative Adversarial Networks (GANs) which can enlarge the existing datasets with more low-cost generated samples.

2.2 Generative Adversarial Networks

Generative Adversarial Networks (GANs), which were first proposed by [11], have shown a strong ability to generate fake but convincing samples in many domains. Lots of architecture variants, including DCGANs [22], LAPGANs [8], and BEGANs [3], have been proposed to support stabilization of the training process or to improve the generation quality for GANs. Nowadays, GANs are widely applied in a variety of intelligent tasks, such as image manipulation [31], texture synthesis [2], and semantic segmentation [30].

Nevertheless, existing generation models of HAR tasks mainly applied Recurrent Networks or LSTM [1], which are seemingly competent because these architectures permit internal updates of time-series state memory. [27] proposed SensoryGAN, a unified structure of GANs that generates accelerator-based HAR data with a mixture of convolutional and recurrent neurons. Authors transform tri-variate time series of an accelerometer into an one-dimensional representation of vector distance. However, their approach solely adopts LSTM structures and one-dimension Convolutional Neural Networks (1D-CNN), which are unable to capture the intrinsic cross-axis relationship between the sensor-based data distribution of the three different axes of the accelerometer. In [29], authors proposed SenseGAN, a semi-supervised framework for leveraging unlabelled sensor-based data to reduce the negative effect of data scarcity on a classifier's training process. However, their approach lacks visual inspections or quality evaluations on generated samples. [15] use GAN to learn and generate more human pose pictures, but their approach is not applicable to sensor-based HAR datasets that are composed of multi-channel time-series signals. [10,19] address the usage of LSTM-based GANs on HAR under different scenarios, but these structures are not competent when we want the generator to learn the cross-axis feature representations or correlations among X-Y-Z axes from the accelerometer data.

We can see from existing works that, for now, there still lacks investigation on GAN-based approaches for generating sensor-based fine-grained hand activities. Furthermore, the use of convolution-based GAN in HAR is less addressed, making it incompetent to capture the intrinsic relations among sensor axis.

3   GAN-Based Data Augmentation

In this section, we introduce how we transform the data from temporal sequence into multi-dimensional tensor and we describe our GAN-based framework for data augmentation.

3.1   Data Transformation

The accelerator-based hand activity dataset opensourced by [17], whose labels are shown in Table 1, captures both gross orientation and movement of the hands which contains bio-acoustic information of hand activities. To be specific, the original IMU data collected is of 256-unit length recorded by 3-axis accelerometer (X, Y and Z axes) at 4 kHz. Such sampling rate with a buffer of 8192 samples supports the data processing by Fourier transforms (4096 bins with a 0.5 Hz resolution). Since most signals of hand activities are distributed around the lowest 256 FFT bins representing frequencies from 0–128 Hz, these 256 bins are saved into a 48-frame rolling spectrogram, representing a total 3 s of activity signals. By this pre-processing, the 1-D accelerometer signals are now stacked as 256 frequency bins × 48 frames × 3 orientations. Since CNN has been shown well capable on multi-channel vision datasets (Height × Width × RGB Channels), this up-dimensional transformation enables our CNN-based GAN architecture to learn cross-axis relationships which are eliminated by other approaches where three orientation channels are added up to become a one-dimensional sequence. After this up-dimensional transformation, we can even visualize these signal samples in RGB mode like pictures as shown in Fig. 1. However, since this visualization is not human-readable, in the following sections we provide several ways to further evaluate and interpret these samples.

Table 1. Label information of hand activities.

Index Label	0	1	2	3	4	5
Activity Name	Brushing Hair	Brushing Teeth	Chopping Vegetables	Clapping	Drinking	Grating
Index Label	6	7	8	9	10	11
Activity Name	Hands Still - Idle	Moving-Clicking Mouse	Opening Door	Opening Jar	Operating Hand Drill	Petting

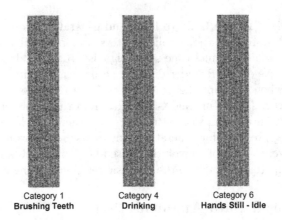

Category 1   Category 4   Category 6
Brushing Teeth   Drinking   Hands Still - Idle

Fig. 1. Visualizing transformed signal instances in RGB mode.

3.2 Architecture Description

Min-Max Optimization. Inspired by [22], we apply a 2D-Convolution-based GAN structure to generate more synthetic 2D-form hand activity signals to augment the original dataset. As we show in Eq. 1 which is basically a min-max optimization process of population risk, the generator $\mathcal{G}$ attempts to generate samples that fool the discriminator $\mathcal{D}$ while the latter is updating parameters to better distinguish between real and fake samples correctly. In the end, the generator should be able to simulate a distribution that is close enough to the distribution of real data to beat the discriminator.

$$\min_{\mathcal{G}} \max_{\mathcal{D}} \mathcal{L}(\mathcal{D}, \mathcal{G}) = \\ \mathbb{E}_{x \sim p_{data}(x)}[\log \mathcal{D}(x)] + \mathbb{E}_{z \sim p_z(z)}[\log(1 - \mathcal{D}(\mathcal{G}(z)))] \tag{1}$$

In Eq. 1, x is the real input sample from original dataset and z is the random Gaussian noise with a certain starting seed. Our working pipeline is shown in Algorithm 1.

The Generator. The generator uses Conv2DTranspose-LeakyReLU blocks to generate the target 2D-format signals by gradually up-sampling from a random noise. The final generated result is of the size (256, 48, 3). Instead of the theoretical population risk, in practice we let the generator to minimize the empirical risk $\mathcal{L}_\mathcal{G}$ in Eq. 2.

$$\mathcal{L}_\mathcal{G} = \frac{1}{m} \sum_{i=1}^{m} \log(1 - \mathcal{D}(\mathcal{G}(z_i))) \tag{2}$$

In the equation above, m denotes for the number of training instances. The structure of generator is shown in Fig. 2.

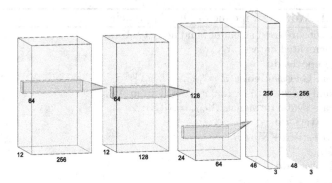

Fig. 2. The architecture of our approach's generator.

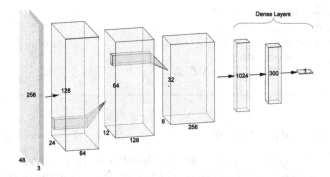

Fig. 3. The architecture of our approach's discriminator.

The Discriminator. The discriminator contains Conv2D-LeakyReLU blocks such that this convolution-based structure will take in a tensor of the size (256, 48, 3) to classify the input samples as real (prediction of 1) or fake (prediction of 0). Similar to the generator, in practice we let the discriminator to minimize the empirical risk $\mathcal{L}_{\mathcal{D}}$ in Eq. 3.

$$\mathcal{L}_{\mathcal{D}} = \frac{1}{m} \sum_{i=1}^{m} \log \mathcal{D}(x_i) + \log(1 - \mathcal{D}(\mathcal{G}(z_i))) \tag{3}$$

The structure of discriminator is shown in Fig. 3. The filter window size of all convolution layers in both generator and discriminator is (5, 5).

4   Experiments and Analysis

In this section, we generate synthetic data following our proposed approach. Then we conduct experiments to evaluate the improvement of the classifier's test accuracy by training on the augmented dataset (i.e., real+synthetic data). We also propose several ways of data visualization to visually assess and analyse the synthetic data of different labels.

Algorithm 1. Working Pipeline of Our Approach

Input: Real sensor-based signal of hand activity $\mathcal{X}_{hand}$.
Output: Augmented dataset $\mathcal{X}_{aug}$.
1: **for** N_{GAN} epochs **do**
2:     Random Gaussian noise $\mathcal{Z} = \{z_0, z_1, .., z_m\}$;
3:     Randomly pick $\mathcal{X}_{real} = \{x_0, x_1, .., x_m\}$ from X_{hand};
4:     Generate synthetic signals $\mathcal{X}_{fake} = \mathcal{G}(\mathcal{Z})$;
5:     **for** S_D steps **do**
6:         $W_D \leftarrow W_D + \nabla_D \mathcal{L}_D$;
7:     **end for**
8:     **for** S_G steps **do**
9:         $W_G \leftarrow W_G - \nabla_G \mathcal{L}_G$;
10:     **end for**
11: **end for**
12: New random Gaussian noise $\mathcal{Z}_{new}$;
13: Synthetic data $\mathcal{X}_{gen} = \mathcal{G}(\mathcal{Z}_{new})$;
14: Augmented dataset $\mathcal{X}_{aug} = \mathcal{X}_{hand} \cup \mathcal{X}_{gen}$;
15: **for** $N_{Classifier}$ epochs **do**
16:     $W_{Classifier} = W_{Classifier} - \nabla\mathcal{L}_{classifier}$;
17: **end for**

4.1 Implementation Details

The training of our GAN and hand classifier baseline (called Hand-12 in Sect. 4.2) uses a GPU cluster of NVIDIA GeForce RTX 2080 Ti. During the training of generator and discriminator, we set 200 epochs with the batch size of 256 samples. The generator and discriminator's optimizers in our approach are both Adam with the learning rate of 0.0001. After training, there are multiple generator-discriminator pairs, each for one category of hand activity. During the training of Hand-12 DCNN classifier, we set 100 epochs with the batch size of 64 samples. The optimizer for Hand-12 is Adam with the learning rate of 0.001. In the generation of synthetic data, we train generators on each category (around 3500 training instances) and generate 4,000 more instances for each category.

4.2 Improving Classifier's Performance

We refer to the VGG-vriant classifier proposed by [17], namely Hand-24, that is specifically designed for sensor-based hand activity recognition with a DCNN structure. To fit our 12-category situation, we deploy a modified version of this approach, Hand-12, shown in Fig. 4, where the number of neurons in dense layers are slightly reduced. This reduction yields to an increase in baseline accuracy from 90.70% to 91.76%. To be specific, we train the Hand-12 on the original training set (round 1 to round 3 in the dataset), which is a collection of 12 categories of hand activities (y label index 0 to index 11), then we test the model on the original test set (round 4 in the dataset).

Table 2. Categorical test accuracy of Hand-12 after training on augmented (12 × 2K).

Activity label	All	0	1	2	3	4	5	6	7	8	9	10	11
Test samples	14973	1225	1248	1251	1201	1250	1253	1248	1253	1249	1255	1254	1286
Test accuracy	0.9419	0.9894	0.9583	0.9041	1.0000	1.0000	0.9832	0.9944	0.9162	0.8319	0.8351	1.0000	0.8950

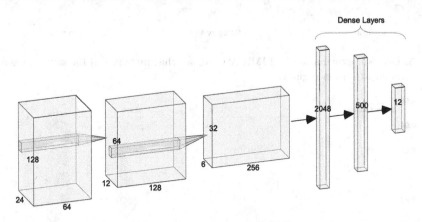

Fig. 4. The architecture of Hand-12.

After obtaining generated activity samples for each category, we mix them with the original training set to have augmented datasets of different ratios between real and synthetic data. To evaluate that different amounts of augmentation will have different effects on the training, we train the baseline on the following settings in which the original training set (44862 instances) is augmented with: 1 category of 2K synthetic data (46862 instances), 12 categories of 1K synthetic data (56862 instances), 12 categories of 2K synthetic data (68862 instances), 12 categories of 4K synthetic data (92862 instances). Table 2 shows the classification test accuracy on each category of data after we train the baseline model on augmented training set (68862 instances). The comparison results of accuracy improvement of every different setting are shown in Fig. 6. We were able to see that the dataset augmented with 12 categories of 2K synthetic data (68862 instances) had the highest test accuracy compared to other settings. This shows that our approach to augment the original training set can help the classifier to better fit the data distribution and hence perform better on the test set. Note that the setting of 12 categories of 4K synthetic data (92862 instances) has a slightly lower test accuracy compared to 12 × 2k. We believe that this is because, when the augmented part highly outnumbers the original training set, the classifier may not be able to best fit the original distribution. But despite the small drop compared to 12 × 2k, the 12 × 4k setting still outperforms the original setting.

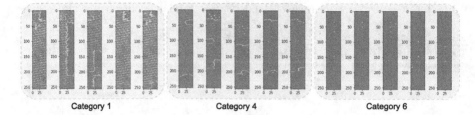

Fig. 5. Decision explanation by LIME. We can see that instances of the same category share similar attention regions.

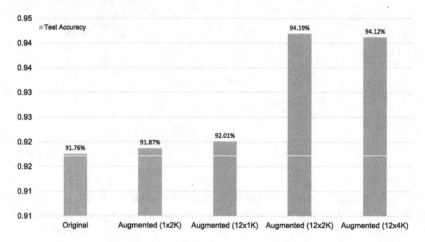

Fig. 6. Overall test accuracy improvements by dataset augmentation.

4.3   Data Visualization

Unlike natural pictures, we cannot simply visualize the samples of size (256, 48, 3) by RGB mode shown in Fig. 1 because there are no observed distinguishable features. Although it is hard to classify these signal instance by the human eye, we propose two ways to visualize the samples and enable feature interpretation, namely Axis-Wise Heatmap and Interpretation with Classifier's Attention. Due to the restriction of page limit, we only demonstrate visualizing instances of 3 categories: brushing teeth, drinking, and hand still idle.

Axis-Wise Heatmap. Considering each axis of the instance is a matrix of floating numbers, we found that heatmap-based visualization of each axis separately can enable rough classification by human observation. Shown in Fig. 7 as a demonstration, we decompose each instance given in Fig. 1 by 3 axis, then we normalize each matrix (axis of size (256, 48, 1)) and visualize them as heatmaps. A darker pixel indicates a higher sensor-based value. As we can see, each axis of the example instance of category 1 is denser and darker at bottom while being sparse at top of the matrices. Inversely, the instance of category 4 is sparser at

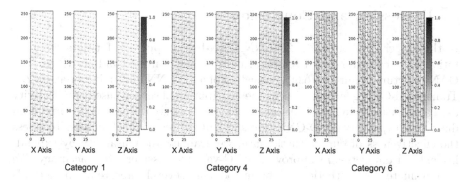

Fig. 7. Axis-wise heatmap.

bottom while the pixels are denser at top. Since category 6 is hand still (idle), we can see that its axis-based heatmaps are repeating similar textures from top to bottom and it does not show significant differences in the attention masks. It is therefore distinguishable from the other two category.

Interpretation with Classifier's Attention. In contrast to axis-separated evaluations, it is also feasible to analyse the three-dimensional signal instance as a whole by explaining the predictions of its DCNN classifier. More specifically, the latent evidence that helps the classifier to classify samples with different labels can be helpful for sample visualization. To make such latent contribution distinguishable for human observation, we implement Local Interpretable Model-agnostic Explanations (LIME) [23] to explain the most contributing features in the input samples of the augmented dataset for our Hand-12 DCNN classifier. To the best of our knowledge, we are the first to use such an assessment method in sensor-based hand activity recognition. Shown in Fig. 5 as a demonstration, for each category, we take two correctly-classified instances from the original dataset and three correctly-classified instances from the synthetic dataset, then we apply LIME to explain the classification of Hand-12. As can be seen, the instances of the same category share some common features that are masked by the assessment method. For example, in category 4, although the top areas are slightly different, all instances' bottom area are masked as contributing features. Moreover, in category 1, although different at the bottom, all instances have a masked area at the top corner. Lastly, in category 6 hand still (idle), it can be observed that nearly all areas contribute equally to the prediction since most areas in the samples are masked. This phenomenon matches our previous observations in the Axis-Wise Heatmap section. In the heatmap, we can also distinguish these categories considering that heatmaps of category 1 are denser at bottom while heatmaps of category 4 are denser at the top.

5 Discussion and Conclusion

In this paper, we propose a 2D-CNN GAN-based approach for data augmentation on accelerator-based temporal data of fine-grained hand activities. The GAN structure in our approach, consisting of a 2D-CNN discriminator and a 2D-Transposed-CNN generator, learns the distribution of sensor-based hand activity data and generates synthetic instances that well reserve the cross-axis correlation due to the capability of 2D-CNN layers learning three-channel tensors. To assess the effectiveness of our synthetic data, we evaluate their usability by expanding existed datasets and improving VGG-variant classifier's test accuracy. We also evaluate the synthetic data by introducing several interpretation methods including axis-wise heatmap and model-oriented explanation. The experiments show that our approach is able to fit on each category of activity data investigated and to effectively improve the classifier's test accuracy by GAN-based data augmentation.

Moving forward, we will focus on (1) utilizing our approach on sensor-based data with conditional label information, (2) exploring more efficient deep architectures for data augmentation and more accurate classifiers for fine-grained hand activity recognition, and (3) developing more interpretation tools for GAN-based data augmentation to make sure that such an approach is reliable and deployable in the real world.

References

1. Alzantot, M., Chakraborty, S., Srivastava, M.: SenseGen: a deep learning architecture for synthetic sensor data generation. In: 2017 IEEE International Conference on Pervasive Computing and Communications Workshops (PerCom Workshops), March 2017. https://doi.org/10.1109/PERCOMW.2017.7917555
2. Bergmann, U., Jetchev, N., Vollgraf, R.: Learning texture manifolds with the periodic spatial GAN (2017)
3. Berthelot, D., Schumm, T., Metz, L.: BEGAN: boundary equilibrium generative adversarial networks. arXiv abs/1703.10717 (2017)
4. Biswas, D., et al.: Cornet: deep learning framework for PPG-based heart rate estimation and biometric identification in ambulant environment. IEEE Trans. Biomed. Circuits Syst. 13(2), 282–291 (2019)
5. Bulling, A., Blanke, U., Schiele, B.: A tutorial on human activity recognition using body-worn inertial sensors. ACM Comput. Surv. 46(3) (2014). https://doi.org/10.1145/2499621
6. Chen, K., Yao, L., Zhang, D., Wang, X., Chang, X., Nie, F.: A semisupervised recurrent convolutional attention model for human activity recognition. IEEE Trans. Neural Netw. Learn. Syst. PP, 1–10 (2019). https://doi.org/10.1109/TNNLS.2019.2927224
7. Chen, K., Zhang, D., Yao, L., Guo, B., Yu, Z., Liu, Y.: Deep learning for sensor-based human activity recognition: overview, challenges and opportunities. arXiv preprint arXiv:2001.07416 (2020)

8. Denton, E.L., Chintala, S., Szlam, A., Fergus, R.: Deep generative image models using a Laplacian pyramid of adversarial networks. In: Cortes, C., Lawrence, N.D., Lee, D.D., Sugiyama, M., Garnett, R. (eds.) Advances in Neural Information Processing Systems 28, pp. 1486–1494. Curran Associates, Inc. (2015)
9. Doan, H.G., Vu, H., Tran, T.H.: Recognition of hand gestures from cyclic hand movements using spatial-temporal features. In: Proceedings of the Sixth International Symposium on Information and Communication Technology, SoICT 2015, pp. 260–267. Association for Computing Machinery, New York (2015). https://doi.org/10.1145/2833258.2833301
10. Gammulle, H., Denman, S., Sridharan, S., Fookes, C.: Multi-level sequence GAN for group activity recognition. In: Jawahar, C.V., Li, H., Mori, G., Schindler, K. (eds.) ACCV 2018. LNCS, vol. 11361, pp. 331–346. Springer, Cham (2019). https://doi.org/10.1007/978-3-030-20887-5_21
11. Goodfellow, I., et al.: Generative adversarial nets. In: Ghahramani, Z., Welling, M., Cortes, C., Lawrence, N.D., Weinberger, K.Q. (eds.) Advances in Neural Information Processing Systems 27, pp. 2672–2680. Curran Associates, Inc. (2014). http://papers.nips.cc/paper/5423-generative-adversarial-nets.pdf
12. Hammerla, N., Fisher, J., Andras, P., Rochester, L., Walker, R., Plötz, T.: PD disease state assessment in naturalistic environments using deep learning. In: Twenty-ninth AAAI Conference on Artificial Intelligence (AAAI-2015). Newcastle University (2015)
13. Huynh, T., Schiele, B.: Analyzing features for activity recognition. In: Proceedings of the 2005 Joint Conference on Smart Objects and Ambient Intelligence: Innovative Context-Aware Services: Usages and Technologies, sOc-EUSAI 2005, pp. 159–163. Association for Computing Machinery, New York (2005). https://doi.org/10.1145/1107548.1107591
14. Khan, S.S., Taati, B.: Detecting unseen falls from wearable devices using channelwise ensemble of autoencoders. Expert Syst. Appl. **87**, 280–290 (2017). https://doi.org/10.1016/j.eswa.2017.06.011
15. Kiasari, M.A., Moirangthem, D.S., Lee, M.: Human action generation with generative adversarial networks. arXiv abs/1805.10416 (2018)
16. Lane, N.D., Georgiev, P.: Can deep learning revolutionize mobile sensing? In: Proceedings of the 16th International Workshop on Mobile Computing Systems and Applications, HotMobile 2015, pp. 117–122. Association for Computing Machinery, New York (2015). https://doi.org/10.1145/2699343.2699349
17. Laput, G., Harrison, C.: Sensing fine-grained hand activity with smartwatches. In: Proceedings of the 2019 CHI Conference on Human Factors in Computing Systems, CHI 2019 pp. 1–13. Association for Computing Machinery, New York (2019). https://doi.org/10.1145/3290605.3300568
18. Luna-Perejon, F., et al.: An automated fall detection system using recurrent neural networks. In: Riaño, D., Wilk, S., ten Teije, A. (eds.) AIME 2019. LNCS (LNAI), vol. 11526, pp. 36–41. Springer, Cham (2019). https://doi.org/10.1007/978-3-030-21642-9_6
19. Moshiri, P., Navidan, H., Shahbazian, R., Ghorashi, S.A., Windridge, D.: Using GAN to enhance the accuracy of indoor human activity recognition. arXiv abs/2004.11228 (2020)
20. Münzner, S., Schmidt, P., Reiss, A., Hanselmann, M., Stiefelhagen, R., Dürichen, R.: CNN-based sensor fusion techniques for multimodal human activity recognition. In: Proceedings of the 2017 ACM International Symposium on Wearable Computers, ISWC 2017, pp. 158–165. Association for Computing Machinery, New York (2017). https://doi.org/10.1145/3123021.3123046

21. Ogata, M., Imai, M.: Skinwatch: skin gesture interaction for smart watch. In: Proceedings of the 6th Augmented Human International Conference, AH 2015, pp. 21–24. Association for Computing Machinery, New York (2015). https://doi.org/10.1145/2735711.2735830
22. Radford, A., Metz, L., Chintala, S.: Unsupervised representation learning with deep convolutional generative adversarial networks (2015)
23. Ribeiro, M.T., Singh, S., Guestrin, C.: "Why should I trust you?": explaining the predictions of any classifier. In: Proceedings of the 22nd ACM SIGKDD International Conference on Knowledge Discovery and Data Mining, San Francisco, CA, USA, 13–17 August 2016, pp. 1135–1144 (2016)
24. Shipman, F.M., Gutierrez-Osuna, R., Monteiro, C.D.D.: Identifying sign language videos in video sharing sites. ACM Trans. Access. Comput. 5(4) (2014). https://doi.org/10.1145/2579698
25. Tu, Y., Lin, Y., Wang, J., Kim, J.U.: Semi-supervised learning with generative adversarial networks on digital signal modulation classification. Comput. Mater. Continua 55(2), 243–254 (2018)
26. Wang, J., Chen, Y., Hao, S., Peng, X., Hu, L.: Deep learning for sensor-based activity recognition: a survey. Pattern Recogn. Lett. 119, 3–11 (2019)
27. Wang, J., Chen, Y., Gu, Y., Xiao, Y., Pan, H.: SensoryGANs: an effective generative adversarial framework for sensor-based human activity recognition. In: 2018 International Joint Conference on Neural Networks (IJCNN), pp. 1–8 (2018)
28. Yang, J.B., Nguyen, M.N., San, P.P., Li, X.L., Krishnaswamy, S.: Deep convolutional neural networks on multichannel time series for human activity recognition. In: Proceedings of the 24th International Conference on Artificial Intelligence, IJCAI 2015, pp. 3995–4001. AAAI Press (2015)
29. Yao, S., et al.: SenseGan: enabling deep learning for internet of things with a semisupervised framework. Proc. ACM Interact. Mob. Wearable Ubiquit. Technol. 2(3) (2018). https://doi.org/10.1145/3264954
30. Zhang, X., Zhu, X., Zhang, X., Zhang, N., Li, P., Wang, L.: SegGAN: semantic segmentation with generative adversarial network. In: 2018 IEEE Fourth International Conference on Multimedia Big Data (BigMM), pp. 1–5 (2018)
31. Zhu, J.Y., Park, T., Isola, P., Efros, A.A.: Unpaired image-to-image translation using cycle-consistent adversarial networks. In: 2017 IEEE International Conference on Computer Vision (ICCV), pp. 2242–2251 (2017)

Personalization Models for Human Activity Recognition with Distribution Matching-Based Metrics

Huy Thong Nguyen[✉], Hyeokhyen Kwon, Harish Haresamudram,
Andrew F. Peterson, and Thomas Plötz

Georgia Institute of Technology, Atlanta, GA 30332, USA
{huythong,hyeokhyen,harishkashyap,afpeterson,thomas.ploetz}@gatech.edu

Abstract. Building activity recognition systems conventionally involves training a common model from all data of training users and utilizing this model to recognize activities of unseen subjects. However, participants come from diverse demographics, so that different users can perform the same actions in diverse ways. Each subject might exhibit user-specific signal patterns, yet a group of users may perform activities in similar manners and share analogous patterns. Leveraging this intuition, we explore Frechet Inception Distance (FID) as a distribution matching-based metric to measure the similarity between users. From that, we propose the nearest-FID-neighbors and the FID-graph clustering techniques to develop user-specific models that are trained with data from the community the testing user likely belongs to. Verified on a series of benchmark wearable datasets, the proposed techniques significantly outperform the model trained with all users.

1 Introduction

Human activity recognition (HAR), which involves identifying the activities performed by people based on data from body-worn sensors, is at the core of wearable computing. The conventional approach includes training a model from data available from all known participants, and subsequently utilizing these data to predict activities of unseen users. One of the critical observations is that wearable data inherently involve participants from diverse demographics, such as genders, ages, weights, heights, lifestyles. Such diversity of activities across participants necessitates diverse, large-scale data collection which is yet to be realized due to the high costs.

Subsets of the users in a dataset may comprise a number of communities whose users are similar to each other (lower intra-community variability), yet distinct from other communities (higher inter-community variability). Intuitively, a model trained with data from a user community that is more similar to the target user may result in improved performance over using all users. To conceptualize

---

H. T. Nguyen and H. Kwon—Both authors contributed equally to this research.

© Springer Nature Singapore Pte Ltd. 2021
X. Li et al. (Eds.): DL-HAR 2020, CCIS 1370, pp. 43–56, 2021.
https://doi.org/10.1007/978-981-16-0575-8_4

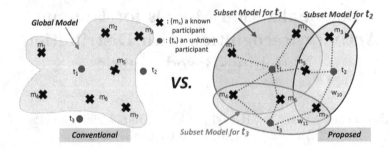

Fig. 1. A conceptual drawing of the conventional and proposed model training approaches. (Color figure online)

the idea in Fig. 1, we depict m_x and t_x representing the known and unknown user representation spaces respectively. The conventional approach trains the global model with all known participants datasets, m_xs, and draws a yellow decision region, and as a result, this global model is likely to have prediction failures for the unknown users out of decision regions, such as t_2, t_3. On the contrary, the personal method identifies the community of training users that are most similar to a testing user and use those data to train personal models to recognize activities on the test user. The subset models are more likely to capture activity patterns similar to the target users, and thus contain more compact and effective decision boundaries, such as red-t_1, blue-t_2, green-t_3 decision boundaries as conceptually depicted in Fig. 1.

In this work, we explore the Frechet Inception Distance (FID) as a distribution matching-based metric to measure similarity between the users, where this FID score has effectively measured the distance between two distributions across various applications [6,8]. From that, we propose two different approaches that are nearest-FID-neighbor or graph clustering-FID-based algorithms to detect multiple subsets where a test user is likely to belong. Evaluated on multiple human activity benchmark datasets, our models significantly outperform the global model that naively trains on all users. We also extensively evaluate the practical scenarios where we can only ask test users to collect a handful amount of data and show the robustness of the approach even when only a few seconds of target user data is available. Interestingly, the FID-based community also aligned with the demographic groups of the users.

2   Related Work

Here we introduce a number of previous works which proposed user-adaptive models by choosing subsets of participants for model training. Related to the FID metric, we also discuss a number of measures to calculate a distance between two distributions.

2.1   User-Adaptive Models

[20] trained personal models on smartphone datasets and [4] built personalized models for time-series physiologial patient data, both of which train personal models from scratch. [14] proposed the personalized Gaussian Process model for predicting key metrics of Alzheimer' Disease progression by training on all available users then gradually fitting personal models to target users. [21] presented a user-adaptive algorithm for activity recognition based on k-mean clustering to match test data to clusters of training users. All those works demand extensive test user data to develop personal models.

Additionally, several related works have utilized personal information to improve activity recognition models. Employing k-means clustering, [19] clustered users based on surveys, such as ages, ethnicity, and jobs. [12] explicitly use surveys about users as an additional feature to train personal models. [11] additionally utilized the GPS location and lifestyle survey to improve the similarity score. Although effective, the previous approaches typically require personal information of users which might raise have privacy issues.

2.2   Distribution Distance Metrics

Majority of the published works use K-means clustering to group users with similarity, such as [21] and [19]. The simple similarity metric demands intensive test user data to compute effective sub-groups to develop personal models. [11] combines various metrics and measures physical similarity based on the Mahalanobis distance, lifestyle similarity based on Euclidean distance on histogram vectors, and sensor data similarity based on the formula in [15]. However, the combination of similarity measurement is still based on the personal information. In this work, we explore the deep-learning-based metric of Frechet Inception Distance (FID) to measure similarity purely from the sensor data. Developed based on the Inception model (see [18]) and Frechet distance, this deep-learning-based metric has been crucial for evaluation and auto-design of Generative Adversarial Networks (GAN) [6,8].

3   Method

In this article, we apply the DeepConvLSTM model [13] to recognize activities, leverage the deep-learning-based metric of Frechet Inception Distance (FID) to measure similarity, and propose two techniques to detect multiple communities where the test user is likely to belong. First, we briefly introduce FID which measures perceptual distance between two domain distributions that have the same set of C classes, $P_1 \sim (X_1, Y_1)$ and $P_2 \sim (X_2, Y_2)$. From raw samples, we first extract high-level feature representations at the output of the last layer of pretrained deep learning model. For features from each class, we calculate the mean $\mu_{1,c}, \mu_{2,c}$ and variance matrices $\Sigma_{1,c}, \Sigma_{2,c}$, and the FID score is then calculated by summing the Frechet distance between two Gaussian distributions for all classes:

$$FID_{(1,2)} = \sum_{k=c}^{C} FID_{(1,2),c} \quad where,$$

$$FID_{(1,2),c} = ||\mu_1 - \mu_2||^2 + Tr\left(\Sigma_1 + \Sigma_2 - 2(\Sigma_1\Sigma_2)^{1/2}\right)$$

We compute FID scores for wearable data by using the pretrained global model as a feature extractor, which captures general concept of activity task, and utilize a 128-dimension vector from the last LSTM layer of DeepConvLSTM models as the feature representation. Subsequently, we calculate the pairwise user FID scores and utilize those to detect communities.

In this work, we make the reasonable assumption that small labeled samples from test users are recorded. As in practical scenarios, we first deploy the global DeepConvLSTM model, and for each new user, we collect a few labeled samples and adapt the global model into user-specific models by using the FID scores. Under this assumption, we utilize two algorithms to detect training user communities which the new user belongs to: nearest-neighbors and graph clustering.

Nearest-FID-Neighbor. We calculate the FID score between all training users and the test user and rank the training users according to FID distances from those to the test user. The community for the test user is constructed by selecting $1 \leq k \leq N$ nearest neighbors from the training users, where N is the maximum number of training users. For the special case when $k = N$, the subset data is equal to the global data. We then train the user specific model on the selected nearest-FID-neighbor training user subsets.

FID-Graph Clustering. From a pairwise FID score between all training users, we generate a graph in which nodes are users and the edge weights are FID scores: $D \in \mathbb{R}^{U \times U}$, where U is the number of training users. To maintain only salient connections between users, we remove edges with an FID score less than the median of all FID scores. From the filtered FID-graph, we apply the Girvan-Newman algorithm [5] to detect meaningful communities with strong connectivities within the graph. Lastly, we select the community as a training set that has the lowest FID score between the test user and community. The FID-graph clustering generates communities relative to the other training users, whereas the nearest-FID-neighbor approach constructs the community in a greedy manner.

4   Experiment

To analyze the effectiveness of our proposed method with various number of participants, we conducted experiments on four publicly available datasets: Opportunity, Daphnet Gait (DG), Wetlab, and Mobiactv2. Recording data from acceleration or guesture sensors, the Opportunity, Daphnet Gait, Wetlab, and Mobiactv2 datasets consists of 4, 10, 21, and 61 participants, respectively.

Opportunity [3] has 18 gesture activities for 4 participants performing kitchen routines such as opening and closing doors, dishwashers, and drawers.

Daphnet Gait dataset [1] includes 10 Parkinson's disease participants experiencing freezing of gait (FoG) while walking.

Wetlab dataset [17] has 8 activities of conducting biology and chemistry experiments on 22 participants.

Mobiact dataset [2] contains data for 11 activities of daily living and 4 types of falls recorded from a smartphone's inertial sensors. Following [7,16], we utilize data for the daily living activities – sitting, walking, jogging, jumping, stairs up, stairs down, stand to sit, sitting on a chair, sit to stand, car step-in, and car step-out, from 61 participants.

Methods. Following previous work [10], we used 1 s window size for Opportunity, DG, and Mobiactv2, 5 s window size for Wetlab, and 0.5 s overlapping was used for all datasets. For classification, we utilize the DeepConvLSTM model [13]. To compensate for label imbalance commonly observed in human activity datasets, weighted cross-entropy loss is utilized to update network parameters. Class weights are set inversely proportional to the number of samples in the classes, $weights \propto 1/N_{data}$, and the mean F1-score is chosen as the metric to compare performance between models.

To facilitate a fair comparison between different training schemes, we train the model for 75 epochs when starting with random initial weights. For models which are finetuned, training is performed only for additional 25 epochs. Those numbers of epochs are large enough to make sure that the loss remains plateau $10 - 15$ epochs before we stop the training. We use the Adam optimizer [9] to update model weights with a fixed learning rate of 0.001 for all datasets. We perform a grid search on the weight decay from $1e-1$ to $1e-5$ and set a decay rate of $1e-5$ for Opportunity, Wetlab, and Mobiactv2 datasets. For the DG dataset, we set it to $1e-2$ in order to avoid overfitting.

Before presenting the results, we define several terms here for clarity. *(i) Global data* refers to the samples from all participants except for the test subject; *(ii) Global model* is the model trained on the global data; *(iii) Global scores* are the mean F1-scores of the global model on the test subjects; *(iv) Subset model* is a model trained on the subset participants present in a community.

5   Results

For each test participant, we compute communities of training participants most similar to the test participant using both the nearest-neighbor and the graph clustering techniques. In what follows, we analyze the performance of both techniques on the benchmark datasets.

5.1   Nearest-FID-Neighbor

In order to evaluate the performance of the nearest-FID-neighbor approach, we first utilize all available data from test users and then analyze the impact of having different amounts of test user data for community detection.

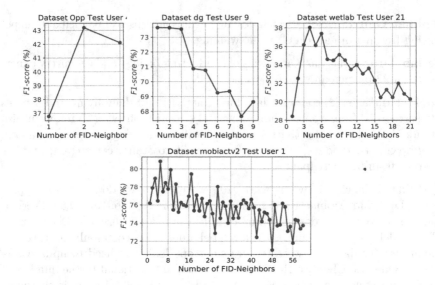

Fig. 2. Experimental results of the nearest-FID-neighbor models as a function of the number of nearest neighbors on various datasets. Typically, the nearest-FID-neighbors subsets with small to medium subset size achieve better performance than the global models. The peak of F1 scores happens at $k = 2$ for test user 3 of Opportunity, $k = 1-3$ for test user 9 of dg, $k = 3 - 7$ for test user 21 of wetlab, $k = 3 - 5$ for test user 1 of mobiactv2 datasets, which demonstrates that the subset models can outperform the global models.

Impact of Neighbor Size. Figure 2 depicts the F1-score of the nearest-FID-neighbor subset models for varying k neighbors across datasets. The F1-score initially improves as we include more nearest FID-neighbors and subsequently rolls down when more distant users are added to the subsets. This clearly demonstrates the existence of more optimal training user subsets such that the performance is improved over using the entire training set.

Opportunity. Figure 3 compares the F1-score of the subset and global models for the Opportunity dataset, which contains 4 participants. Over all possible combinations, we show the best subset results for each test user. When testing on User 3, the subset model $1 + 4$ trained from scratch outperforms the global model by ∼1.5%. The effect of the training dataset size is also shown when subset models are fine-tuned with weights from the global model. For both of the Test Users 1 and 3, subset models outperformed the global models by ∼2.1% and ∼2.9%, respectively, which demonstrating that we can always utilize the global model to adapt to a test user.

Daphnet Freeze of Gait. The Daphnet Freeze of Gait dataset contains 10 participants, and thereby having more subjects than the Opportunity dataset. Figure 4 clearly shows that subset model has more flexibility to find more optimal communities when more participants are available, therefore outperforming

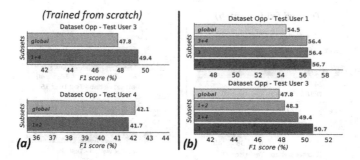

Fig. 3. Subset versus global models for Opportunity dataset (a) trained from scratch (b) fine-tuned from global weights.

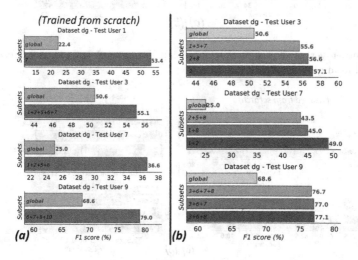

Fig. 4. Subset versus global models for Daphnet Gait dataset. (a) trained from scratch (b) fine-tuned from global weights.

global models even when trained from scratch. For Test User 1, the subset model outperforms the global model by ~21%. Fine-tuning from the global model also drastically boosts the generalization scores. For example, subset models outperform global models by ~6.5% and ~24% for test user 3 and 7, respectively. Running on all test users, the proposed technique improves from the average of all global scores of 46.7% to the average of all nearest-FID-neighbor subset scores of 57.4%, demonstrating 10.7% increase on average.

Wetlab. To simplify naming convention, we use 1–22 to annotate the subjects 101–142 in the Wetlab dataset. Thanks to the availability of many training users, the subset model trained from scratch improves the global scores of 25.4%, 33.1%, and 30.3% to 31.8%, 40.3%, and 36.8% for test user 19, 20, and 21, respectively, as shown in Fig. 5). Also, fine-tuning for global model, subset model for test user 20 could further improve to 43.7%. Evaluating for all test users, the average of

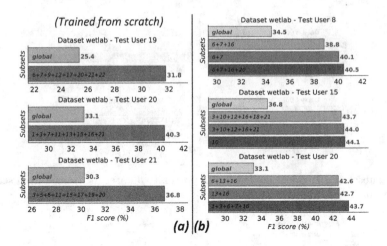

Fig. 5. Subset versus global model for wetlab dataset (a) trained from scratch (b) fine-tuned from global weights.

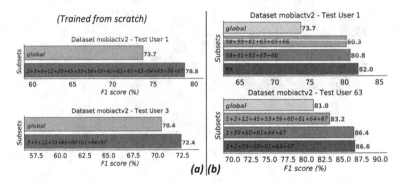

Fig. 6. Subset versus global models for mobiactv2 dataset (a) trained from scratch (b) fine-tuned from global weights.

global scores is 34.6%, while the average of subset scores of 39.5%, demonstrating 4.9% or ×14% improvement for the wetlab dataset.

Mobiactv2. Figure 6 demonstrates the results for the mobiactv2 dataset with 61 participants. Likewise in other datasets, a subset model finetuned from a global model was more effective than training from scratch. For example, the proposed technique improves the F1 score for test user 1 from 73.7% to 78.8%. Fine tunning from global weights for all test users, the average score for subset models is 84.2%, demonstrating 3.5% boost from the average of 80.7% for global scores.

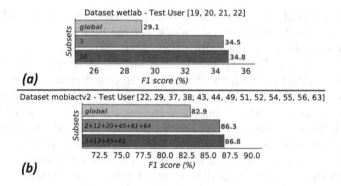

Fig. 7. Subset versus global models for mulitple test users. (a) test sets of wetlab datasets (b) test sets of Mobiactv2 dataset.

Multiple Users. In previous benchmarks, Wetlab and Mobiactv2 datasets evaluated models on the test set consisting of 4 and 13 users, respectively. Shown in Fig. 7, the proposed algorithm improves the scores for multiple test users in wetlab and mobiactv2 from 29.1% to 34.8% and from 82.9% to 86.8%, illustrating an increase of 5.7% and 3.9%, respectively.

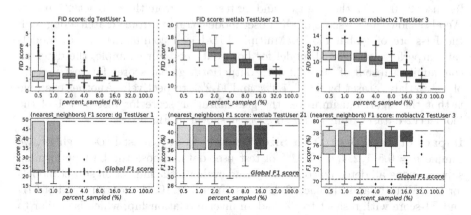

Fig. 8. FID scores (upper) and F1 scores (bottom) versus the varying size of test user data for dg, wetlab, and mobiactv2 dataset with the Nearest-FID-Neighbor algorithm.

Impact of Test User Data Size. In a realistic scenario, the test user's data is not available initially. Although new users can provide a number of annotation samples, we can only ask them to do so for small set of samples practically. Therefore, we analyze the subset model performance when different amounts of test user data is available. We sample $p\%$, where $p = 0.5, 1, 2, 4, 8, 16, 32, 100$, of test user dataset for subset detection, such that the class ration of test user is preserved in sampled data. From the sub-sampled data, we develop the k nearest-FID-neighbor subsets with $k = 3 - 5$ and select the best performing model. For each $p\%$ subsampling, we aggregate results from 500 trials of experiments for statistical significance. For DG, Wetlab, and Mobiactv2 dataset, the results are shown in Fig. 8. As expected, the confidence interval decreases with more test user data for both of FID and F1-score. As $p\%$ increases, the FID scores between the test user and selected community decreases and the F1-score of test user prediction increases. This intuitively shows that the approach is more likely to find the correct community when more test user samples are available. More importantly, as soon as only 0.5% of test user samples are available, the subset models outperform the global models across all datasets, where 0.5% of test user samples equals to 15 s for DG and Wetlab and 10 s for Mobiactv2 dataset. This result is encouraging because asking for less than a minute of data from a new user can be substantial to detect relevant communities for a test user.

5.2   FID-Graph Clustering

Next, we evaluate the performance of FID-graph clustering approach in a similar way as the Nearest-FID-Neighbor. For brevity, we will only show the meaningful results to compare with the Nearest-FID-Neighbor approach.

Graph Community Analysis. In Fig. 9, we depict the FID-based graphs for test user 21 from Wetlab dataset, and for test user 1 from the mobiactv2 dataset. We also show the F1-score of all subset models trained from scratch along with the F1-score of global model. Multiple FID-based community subset models can outperform the global model for both datasets. For example, the detected community subsets of $20 + 22, 3, 19$ outperform global scores for test user 21 of the wetlab dataset by 6.6%, 7.4%, and 11.2%, respectively. Another example is that the algorithm improves the generalization score for test user 1 of the mobiactv2 dataset from 73.7% to 82%, as shown in Fig. 9b.

Impact of Test User Data Size. Similarly from Nearest-FID-Neighbor, we sample $p = 0.5, 1, 2, 4, 8, 16, 32\%$ of test user data, choose the best performing subset among all detected community, and evaluate the impact on subset models for DG, Wetlab, and Mobiactv2 datasets. From Fig. 10, the overall trend of FID and F1-score with respect to $p\%$ had an inverse relationship, which is similar to the case of Nearest-FID-Neighbors. Also, only a small amount 0.5% of test data was enough to build user-adapted models that outperform global models across the datasets.

Demographic Interpretation. The differences in activity patterns between users may come from their demographic differences, such as heights, weights, ages, genders. In Fig. 11, we analyze if the F1-score spectrum of the community subsets carry demographic meanings on the Mobiatcv2 dataset that provides the demographic information of users. The upper spectrum of the community subsets with the highest generalization scores often indicates the similar demographic, while the lower spectrum with the lowest F1 scores frequently suggests the opposite demographic, as demonstrated for User 1 of the Mobiactv2

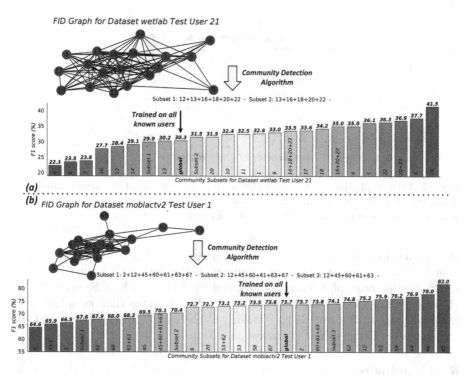

Fig. 9. FID-graph clustering on (a) wetlab (b) mobiactv2 datasets. Typically, the global score lies at the middle of the community spectrum.

dataset. Particularly, User 65, which forms the community with the highest F1 score, shared similar demographic characteristics to User 1, both of which are

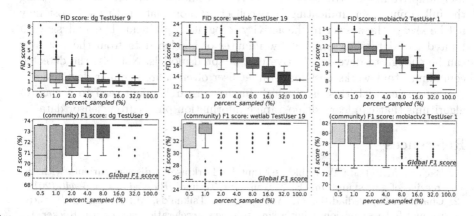

Fig. 10. FID scores (upper) and F1 scores (bottom) versus the varying size of test user data for dg, wetlab, and mobiactv2 dataset with the FID-graph clustering.

Test User 1

ID	Age	Height	Weight	Gender	F1
5	36	160	50	F	64.6%
3	26	164	55	F	66.5%
1	32	180	85	M	--------
66	20	193	83	M	78.0%
65	40	170	100	M	82.0%

Red: Lowest F1 / Green: Highest F1

Fig. 11. FID-graph clustering on the test user 1 of the mobiactv2 dataset and corresponding demographic information. Similar demographic leads to highest F1 scores, while opposite demographic results in lowest F1 scores.

male with similar heights (180 m–170 m) and weights (85 kg–100 kg). In addition, User 5, which represents the community with the lowest F1 score, illustrates contrasting demographic features compared to User 1, such as Female, shorter (160 m), lighter (50 kg) weights. This study demonstrates that we might infer the demographic of a test user by looking at the community spectrum and the corresponding demographic of the communities.

6   Conclusion

When large-scale datasets are not available, carefully selecting most effective training data to build activity recognition models can be more beneficial than naively using the entire datasets to do so. In this work, we proposed algorithms that can select the training user samples that are relevant to a target based on the distribution matching metrics, namely FID score. With our approach, user-adaptive models trained on far less data could be more effective than using the full training set, indicating that collecting more data with more cost may not be always the answer to the activity recognition problem. The analysis with limited test data shows that a few minutes of labeled data from the test user can be enough to develop effective user-adapted models. Notably, the detected community that works best for a target user often shared similar demographic characteristics with this user, which further research might lead to a class of algorithms that can learn demographic information purely from sensor data.

References

1. Bächlin, M., et al.: Wearable assistant for Parkinson's disease patients with the freezing of gait symptom. IEEE Trans. Inf. Technol. Biomed. **14**, 436–446 (2010)
2. Chatzaki, C., Pediaditis, M., Vavoulas, G., Tsiknakis, M.: Human daily activity and fall recognition using a smartphone's acceleration sensor. In: Röcker, C., O'Donoghue, J., Ziefle, M., Helfert, M., Molloy, W. (eds.) ICT4AWE 2016. CCIS, vol. 736, pp. 100–118. Springer, Cham (2017). https://doi.org/10.1007/978-3-319-62704-5_7

3. Chavarriaga, R., et al.: The opportunity challenge: a benchmark database for on-body sensor-based activity recognition. Pattern Recogn. Lett. **23**, 2033–2042 (2013). https://doi.org/10.1016/j.patrec.2012.12.014

4. Clifton, L., Clifton, D., Pimentel, M., Watkinson, P., Tarassenko, L.: Gaussian processes for personalized e-health monitoring with wearable sensors. IEEE Trans. Biomedical Eng. **60**, 193–197 (2013). https://doi.org/10.1109/TBME.2012.2208459

5. Girvan, M., Newman, M.E.J.: Community structure in social and biological networks. Proc. Natl. Acad. Sci. **99**(12), 7821–7826 (2002). https://doi.org/10.1073/pnas.122653799. https://www.pnas.org/content/99/12/7821

6. Gong, X., Chang, S., Jiang, Y., Wang, Z.: AutoGAN: neural architecture search for generative adversarial networks (2019)

7. Haresamudram, H., et al.: Masked reconstruction based self-supervision for human activity recognition. In: Proceedings of the 2020 International Symposium on Wearable Computers, pp. 45–49 (2020)

8. Heusel, M., Ramsauer, H., Unterthiner, T., Nessler, B., Klambauer, G., Hochreiter, S.: GANs trained by a two time-scale update rule converge to a nash equilibrium. CoRR abs/1706.08500 (2017). http://arxiv.org/abs/1706.08500

9. Kingma, D., Ba, J.: Adam: a method for stochastic optimization. In: International Conference on Learning Representations, December 2014

10. Kwon, H., Abowd, G.D., Plötz, T.: Handling annotation uncertainty in human activity recognition. In: Proceedings of the 23rd International Symposium on Wearable Computers, ISWC 2009, pp. 109–117. Association for Computing Machinery, New York (2019). https://doi.org/10.1145/3341163.3347744

11. Lane, N.D., et al.: Community similarity networks. Pers. Ubiquit. Comput. **18**(2), 355–368 (2014). https://doi.org/10.1007/s00779-013-0655-1

12. Liu, D., Peng, F., Shea, A., Rudovic, O., Picard, R.W.: DeepFaceLIFT: interpretable personalized models for automatic estimation of self-reported pain. CoRR abs/1708.04670 (2017). http://arxiv.org/abs/1708.04670

13. Morales, F.J.O., Roggen, D.: Deep convolutional and LSTM recurrent neural networks for multimodal wearable activity recognition. Sensors **16**(1), 115 (2016). http://dblp.uni-trier.de/db/journals/sensors/sensors16.html#MoralesR16

14. Peterson, K., Rudovic, O., Guerrero, R., Picard, R.W.: Personalized gaussian processes for future prediction of Alzheimer's disease progression. CoRR abs/1712.00181 (2017). http://arxiv.org/abs/1712.00181

15. Rubner, Y., Tomasi, C., Guibas, L.: The earth mover's distance as a metric for image retrieval. Int. J. Comput. Vis. **40**, 99–121 (2000). https://doi.org/10.1023/A:1026543900054

16. Saeed, A., Ozcelebi, T., Lukkien, J.: Multi-task self-supervised learning for human activity detection. Proc. ACM Interact. Mob. Wearable Ubiquit. Technol. **3**(2), 1–30 (2019)

17. Scholl, P., Wille, M., Van Laerhoven, K.: Wearables in the wet lab: a laboratory system for capturing and guiding experiments. In: Ubicomp, pp. 589–599. ACM, September 2015. https://doi.org/10.1145/2750858.2807547

18. Szegedy, C., Vanhoucke, V., Ioffe, S., Shlens, J., Wojna, Z.: Rethinking the inception architecture for computer vision. CoRR abs/1512.00567 (2015). http://arxiv.org/abs/1512.00567

19. Taylor, S., Jaques, N., Nosakhare, E., Sano, A., Picard, R.W.: Personalized multi-task learning for predicting tomorrow's mood, stress, and health. IEEE Trans. Affect. Comput. **11**(2), 200–213 (2020). https://doi.org/10.1109/TAFFC.2017.2784832

20. Weiss, G., Lockhart, J.: The impact of personalization on smartphone-based activity recognition. In: AAAI Workshop - Technical Report, January 2012
21. Zhao, S., Li, W., Cao, J.: A user-adaptive algorithm for activity recognition based on k-means clustering, local outlier factor, and multivariate gaussian distribution. Sensors **18**, 1850 (2018). https://doi.org/10.3390/s18061850

Resource-Constrained Federated Learning with Heterogeneous Labels and Models for Human Activity Recognition

Gautham Krishna Gudur[1] and Satheesh Kumar Perepu[2(⊠)]

[1] Global AI Accelerator, Ericsson, Chennai, India
gautham.krishna.gudur@ericsson.com
[2] Ericsson Research, Chennai, India
perepu.satheesh.kumar@ericsson.com

Abstract. One of the most significant applications in pervasive computing for modeling user behavior is Human Activity Recognition (HAR). Such applications necessitate us to characterize insights from multiple resource-constrained user devices using machine learning techniques for effective personalized activity monitoring. On-device Federated Learning proves to be an extremely viable option for distributed and collaborative machine learning in such scenarios, and is an active area of research. However, there are a variety of challenges in addressing statistical (non-IID data) and model heterogeneities across users. In addition, in this paper, we explore a new challenge of interest – to handle *heterogeneities in labels (activities)* across users during federated learning. To this end, we propose a framework with two different versions for federated label-based aggregation, which leverage overlapping information gain across activities – one using *Model Distillation Update*, and the other using *Weighted α-update*. Empirical evaluation on the Heterogeneity Human Activity Recognition (HHAR) dataset (with four activities for effective elucidation of results) indicates an average deterministic accuracy increase of at least ∼11.01% with the model distillation update strategy and ∼9.16% with the weighted α-update strategy. We demonstrate the on-device capabilities of our proposed framework by using Raspberry Pi 2, a single-board computing platform.

Keywords: Human Activity Recognition · On-device deep learning · Federated learning · Heterogeneous labels · Heterogeneous models · Knowledge distillation

1 Introduction

Contemporary machine learning, particularly deep learning has led to major breakthroughs in various domains, such as vision, speech, Internet of Things (IoT), etc. Particularly, on-device deep learning has spiked up a huge interest in the research community owing to their automatic feature extraction mechanisms

© Springer Nature Singapore Pte Ltd. 2021
X. Li et al. (Eds.): DL-HAR 2020, CCIS 1370, pp. 57–69, 2021.
https://doi.org/10.1007/978-981-16-0575-8_5

and the compute capabilities vested in resource-constrained mobile and wearable devices. Sensors embedded in such IoT devices have a vast amount of incoming data which have massive potential to leverage such on-device machine learning techniques on-the-fly to transform them into meaningful information coupled with supervised, unsupervised and/or other learning mechanisms. Human Activity Recognition (HAR) in such personalized IoT devices is a technique of significant importance for our community as it plays a key role in modeling user behavior across a variety of applications like pervasive health monitoring, fitness tracking, fall detection, etc. With the ubiquitous proliferation of such personalized IoT devices, collaborative and distributed learning is now more possible than ever to help best utilize the behavioral information learnt from multiple devices.

However, such collaborative data sharing across devices might always not be feasible owing to privacy concerns from multiple participants. Users might not have any interest in sending their private data to a remote server/cloud, particularly in areas like healthcare. With the advent of *Federated Learning (FL)* [1,17], it is now possible to effectively train a global/centralized model without compromising on sensitive data of various users by enabling the transfer of model weights and updates from local devices to the cloud, instead of conventionally transferring the sensitive data to the cloud. A server has the role of coordinating between models, however most of the work is not performed by a central entity anymore, but by a federation of clients/devices. The *Federated Averaging (FedAvg)* algorithm was first proposed by McMahan et al. in [17] which combines local Stochastic Gradient Descent (SGD) of each client (local device) with a server that aggregates the model weights. Federated learning has been an active and challenging area of research in solving problems pertaining to secure communication protocols, optimization, privacy preserving networks, etc. [14].

Federated Learning deals with various forms of heterogeneities like device, system, statistical heterogeneities, etc. [14]. Particularly in Federated Learning with IoT scenarios, statistical heterogeneities have gained much visibility as a research problem predominantly owing to the non-IID (non-independent and identically distributed) nature of the vast amounts of streaming real-world data incoming from distinct distributions across devices. This leads to challenges in personalized federation of devices, and necessitates us to address various heterogeneities in data and learning processes for effective model aggregation.

An important step in this direction is the ability of end-users to have the choice of architecting their own models, rather than being constrained by the pre-defined architectures mandated by the global model. One effective way to circumvent this problem is by leveraging the concept of knowledge distillation [8], wherein the disparate local models distill their respective knowledge into various *student models* which have a common model architecture, thereby effectively incorporating model independence and heterogeneity. This was proposed by Li et al. in FedMD [13]. However, as much independence and heterogeneity in architecting the users' own models is ensured in their work, *they do not guarantee heterogeneity and independence in labels across users.*

Many such scenarios with heterogeneous labels and models exist in federated IoT settings, such as behaviour/health monitoring, activity tracking, keyword spotting, next-word prediction, etc. Few works address handling new labels in typical machine learning scenarios, however, to the best of our knowledge, there is no work which addresses this important problem of *label and model heterogeneities* in non-IID federated learning scenarios.

The main scientific contributions in this work are as follows:

- Enabling end-users to build and characterize their own preferred local architectures in a federated learning scenario for HAR, so that effective transfer learning and federated aggregation happens between global and local models.
- A framework with two different versions to allow flexible heterogeneous selection of activity labels by showcasing scenarios with and without overlap across different user devices, thereby leveraging the information learnt across devices pertaining to those overlapped activities.
- Empirical demonstration of the framework's ability to handle real-world disparate data/label distributions (non-IID) on-device independent of users on a public HAR dataset, capable of running on simple mobile and wearable devices.

2   Related Work

Deep learning for HAR, particularly inertial/sensor-based HAR measured from devices like accelerometer, gyroscope, etc. for improving pervasive healthcare has been an active area of research [7,18]. Particularly, mobile- and wearable-based deep learning techniques for HAR have proven to be an extremely fruitful area of research with neural network models being able to efficiently run on such resource-constrained devices [12,22,23]. Few other challenges with deep learning for HAR have been explored like handling unlabeled data using semi-supervised and active learning mechanisms [6,24], domain adaptation [2], few-shot learning [4], and many more.

Federated Learning has contributed vividly in enabling distributed and collective machine learning across various such devices. Federated learning and differentially private machine learning have, or soon will emerge to become the de facto mechanisms for dealing with sensitive data, data protected by Intellectual Property rights, GDPR, etc. [1]. Federated Learning was first introduced in [17], and new challenges and open problems to be solved [14] and multiple advancements [9] have been proposed and addressed in many interesting recent works.

Multiple device and system heterogeneities making them optimization problems are addressed in [15]. Personalized federated learning closely deals with optimizing the degree of personalization and contribution from various clients, thereby enabling effective aggregation as discussed in [3]. Federated learning on the edge with disparate data distributions – non-IID data, and creating a small subset of data globally shared between all devices is discussed in [25].

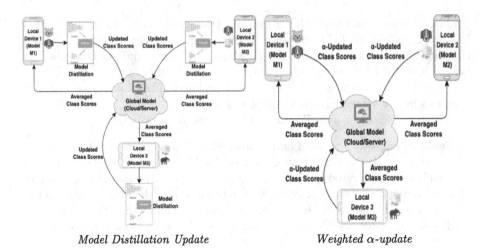

Model Distillation Update   *Weighted α-update*

Fig. 1. Overall architecture with both proposed versions. Each device consists of disparate sets of local labels and models, and they interact with the global model (cloud/server). The models in each local device are first updated using one of the two strategies, the respective class scores are then aggregated in the global model, and the updated consensus is again distributed across local models.

Particularly for Federated Learning in IoT and pervasive (mobile or wearable) devices, important problems and research directions on mobile and edge networks are addressed in this survey [16], while federated optimization for on-device applications is discussed in [11]. Federated Learning for HAR is addressed in [20] which deals with activity sensing with a smart service adapter, while [19] compares between centralized and federated learning approaches.

FedMD [13], which we believe to be our most closest work, deals with heterogeneities in model architectures, and addresses this problem using transfer learning and knowledge distillation [8], and also uses an initial public dataset across all labels (which can be accessed by any device during federated learning). Current federated learning approaches predominantly handle same labels across all the users and do not provide the flexibility to handle unique labels. However, in many practical applications, having unique labels for each local client/model is a very viable scenario owing to their dependencies and constraints on specific regions, demographics, privacy constraints, etc. A version of the proposed work is discussed for vision tasks in [5]. However, to the best of our knowledge, none of the works take into account label and model heterogeneities in the context of HAR.

The rest of the paper is organized as follows. Section 3.1 discusses the problem formulation of handling heterogeneous labels and models in on-device federated learning scenarios, and Sect. 3.2 presents the overall proposed framework and the methods used to address these challenges. Systematic experimentation and evaluation of the framework across different users, devices, iterations, models, activities in a federated learning setting is showcased in Sect. 4, while also proving feasibility of the same on resource-constrained devices (Sect. 4.2). Finally, Sect. 5 concludes the paper.

3   Our Approach

In this section, we discuss in detail about the problem formulation of heterogeneity in labels and models, and our proposed framework to handle the same (showcased in Figs. 1a and 1b).

3.1   Problem Formulation

We assume the following scenario in federated learning. There are multiple local devices which can characterize different model architectures based on the end users. We hypothesize that the incoming data to different devices also consist of heterogeneities in labels, with either unique or overlapping labels. We also have a public dataset with the label set consisting of all labels – this can be accessed by any device anytime, and acts as an initial template of the data and labels that can stream through, over different iterations. We re-purpose this public dataset as the test set also, so that consistency is maintained while testing. To make FL iterations independent from the public dataset, we do not expose the public dataset during learning (training) to the local models. The research problem here is to create a unified framework to handle heterogeneous labels, models and data distributions (non-IID nature) in a federated learning setting.

3.2   Proposed Framework

Our proposed framework to handle heterogeneous labels and models in a federated learning setting is presented in Algorithm 1. There are three important steps in our proposed method.

1. **Build**: In this step, we build the model on the incoming data we have in each local user, i.e., local private data for the specific iteration. The users can choose their own model architecture which suits best for the data present in that iteration.
2. **Local Update**: In this step, we update the averaged global model scores (on public data) for the ith iteration on the local private data. For the first iteration, we do not have any global scores and we initialize the scores to be zero in this case. For the rest of iterations, we have global averaged scores which we can use to update the local model scores according to Algorithm 1. We propose two versions in the local update.
   (a) **Model Distillation Update**, where the local model is distilled based only on labels corresponding to the local user. Distillation acts a summarization of the information captured from the older models in different FL iterations.

Algorithm 1. Our Proposed Framework (with two version choices)

Input: Public Dataset $\mathcal{D}_0\{x_0, y_0\}$, Private Datasets $\mathcal{D}_m^i$, Total users M, Total iterations I, LabelSet l_m for each user

Output: Trained Model scores f_G^I

Initialize $f_G^0 = \mathbf{0}$ (Global Model Scores)

for $i = 1$ to I do

    for $m = 1$ to M do

        Build: Model $\mathcal{D}_m^i$ and predict $f_{\mathcal{D}_m^i}(x_0)$

        Local Update:

        Choice 1 – Model Distillation Update:

        Build a distilled model on only labels corresponding to local user's model with global averaged probabilities on public dataset D_0. Now, update the model with the new data $\mathcal{D}_m^i$ arriving in this iteration.

        Choice 2 – Weighted α-update:

        $f_{\mathcal{D}_m^i}(x_0) = f_G^I(x_0^{l_m}) + \alpha f_{\mathcal{D}_m^i}(x_0)$, where $f_G^I(x_0^{l_m})$ are the global scores of only the set of labels l_m with the mth user, $\alpha = \frac{len(\mathcal{D}_m^i)}{len(\mathcal{D}_0)}$

    end for

    Global Update: Update label wise

    $f_G^{i+1} = \sum_{m=1}^{M} \beta_m f_{\mathcal{D}_m^i}(x_0)$, where

    $\beta = \begin{cases} 1 & \text{If labels are unique} \\ acc(f_{\mathcal{D}_m^{i+1}}(x_0)) & \text{if labels are not unique} \end{cases}$

    where $acc(f_{\mathcal{D}_m^{i+1}}(x_0))$ is the accuracy function of the given model, and is defined by the ratio of correctly classified samples to the total samples for the given local model

end for

(b) **Weighted α-update**, where α is the ratio between the size of current private dataset and the size of public dataset. This parameter governs the contributions of the new and the old models across different FL iterations.

3. **Global update:** In this step, we first train the local model on the respective private datasets for that FL iteration. Further, we evaluate (test) this trained model on the public data, thereby obtaining the model scores on public data. We then perform such label-based averaging across all the users using the β parameter, where β governs the weightage given to unique and overlapping labels across users using test accuracies of the corresponding labels on public data (as given in Algorithm 1). This module gives the global averaged scores.

4   Experiments and Results

We simulate a federated learning scenario with multiple iterations of small chunks of incremental data incoming (details in Table 1), across three different users to test our approach, and assume that the activities arrive in real-time in the users' devices. We use the *Heterogeneity Human Activity Recognition dataset*

Table 1. Model Architectures (filters/units in each layer), Labels (Activities) and Number of Activity Windows per federated learning iteration across user devices. Note the disparate model architectures and labels across users.

	User_1	User_2	User_3	Global_User
Architecture	2-Layer CNN (16, 32) Softmax Activation	3-Layer CNN (16, 16, 32) ReLU Activation	3-Layer ANN (16, 16, 32) ReLU Activation	-
Activities	{Sit, Walk}	{Walk, Stand}	{Stand, StairsUp}	{Sit, Walk, Stand, StairsUp}
Activity Windows per iteration	{2000, 2000} = 4000	{2000, 2000} = 4000	{2000, 2000} = 4000	{2000, 2000, 2000, 2000} = 8000

[21], which consists of inertial data from four different mobile phones across nine users performing six daily activities: Biking, Sitting, Standing, Walking, Stairs-Up, Stairs-Down in heterogeneous conditions.

Data Preprocessing: In this experiment, we perform similar preprocessing techniques as stated in [22]. As discussed, we use the mobile phone accelerometer data only and not gyroscope, due to the reduction in data size without substantial accuracy decrease. We initially segment the triaxial accelerometer data into two-second non-overlapping windows and then perform *Decimation* to downsample (normalize) all activity windows to the least sampling frequency (50 Hz). Following this, Discrete Wavelet Transform (DWT) is performed for obtaining temporal and frequency information and we use Approximation coefficients only, all together is stated to have a substantial decrease in data size.

Now, we discuss the settings for label and model heterogeneities in our experiment.

Label Heterogeneities: In our experiment, we consider only four activities – {*Sit, Walk, Stand, StairsUp*} from the dataset as shown in Table 1. Also, we include the number of activity windows considered per user per iteration (2000 activity windows per iteration). The activities in each local user can either be unique (present only in that single user) or overlapping across users (present in more one user). We split the four activities into three pairs of two activities each, for convenience of showcasing the advantage of overlapping activities in experimentation. We also create a non-IID environment across different federated learning iterations wherein, the activity data across different iterations are split with disparities in both the aforementioned labels and distributions in data (*Statistical Heterogeneities*).

Model Heterogeneities: We choose three different model architectures (CNNs and ANNs) for the three different local users. This is clearly elucidated in Table 1. We also use a simple two-layer ANN model with (8, 16) filters as the

Table 2. Details of Model Architectures (filters/units in each layers) changed across federated learning iterations and users.

Iteration	New model architecture
User_1 Iteration_10	3-Layer ANN (16, 16, 32) ReLU Activation
User_1 Iteration_14	1-Layer CNN (16) Softmax Activation
User_2 Iteration_6	3-Layer CNN (16, 16, 32) Softmax activation
User_3 Iteration_5	4-Layer CNN (8, 16, 16, 32) Softmax activation

distilled student architecture. To truly showcase near-real-time heterogeneity and model independence, we induce a change in the model architectures across and within various FL iterations as shown in Table 2.

Initially, we divide the activity windows across the three different users according to the four activity labels. We create a Public Dataset (D_0) with 8000 activity windows, with 2000 activity windows corresponding to each activity. Next, we sample 2000 activity windows in every iteration for each label of a user (as shown in Table 1). In total, we ran 15 federated learning iterations in this whole experiment, with each iteration running with early stopping (with a maximum 5 epochs). We track the loss using categorical cross-entropy loss function for multi-class classification, and use the Adam optimizer [10] to optimize the classification loss. We simulate all our experiments – both federated learning and inference on a *Raspberry Pi 2*.

Table 3. Average Accuracies (%) of Local and Global Updates, and their respective Accuracy increase with *Model Distillation Update* and *Weighted α-update*.

	Model Distillation			Weighted α-update		
	Local_Update	Global_Update	Increase	Local_Update	Global_Update	Increase
User_1	68.38	77.61	9.23	66.98	74.29	7.31
User_2	70.82	84.4	13.58	68.88	81.9	13.02
User_3	77.68	87.9	10.22	76.57	83.7	7.13
Average	**72.293**	**83.303**	**11.01**	**70.81**	**79.963**	**9.153**

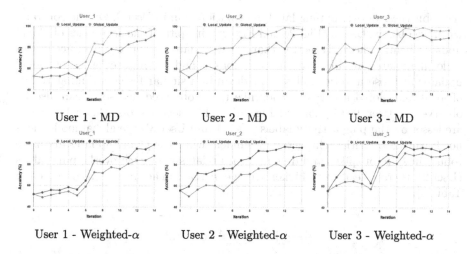

Fig. 2. Iterations vs Accuracy across all three users with *Model Distillation Update* (MD) and *Weighted α-update*. *Local_Update* signifies the accuracy of each local updated model (after i^{th} iteration) on Public Dataset. *Global_Update* signifies the accuracy of the corresponding global updated model (averaged across all the users after i^{th} iteration) on Public Dataset.

4.1   Discussion on Results

Figure 2 represents the results across all three users for both proposed versions of our framework on the HHAR dataset. Also, from Table 3, we can clearly observe that the global updates – which represent the accuracy of the global updated model (and averaged across all users' labels in the ith iteration governed by β), are higher for all three users than the accuracies of their respective local updates. For instance, from Figs. 2a and 2d, we can infer that the corresponding accuracies of labels {*Sit, Walk*} (User 1 labels) after global updates in each iteration are deterministically higher than their respective local updates by an average of ~9.23% and ~7.31% across all iterations with model distillation and α-update versions respectively. Similarly for User 2 labels consisting of {*Walk, Stand*}, we observe an average accuracy increase of ~13.58% and ~13.02% respectively from local updates to the global updates, while for User 3 labels consisting of {*Stand, StairsUp*}, we observe an average increase of ~10.22% and ~7.13% respectively from local updates to global updates in model distillation and α-update versions.

We would like to particularly point out that the overlap in activities significantly contributes to highest increase in accuracies, since information gain (weighted global update) happens only for overlapping labels. This is vividly visible in User 2 (Fig. 2b and Fig. 2e), whose labels are {*Walk, Stand*}), where, in spite of an accuracy dip in local update at FL iterations 5 and 12, the global update at those iterations do not take a spike down which can be primarily attributed to the information gain from overlapping activity labels between User 1 and User 3 (in this case, *Walk* and *Stand* respectively), thereby showcasing the robustness of overlapping label information gain in User 2. On the contrary, when we observe User 3 (Fig. 2c and Fig. 2f), in spite of the accuracies of global updates being inherently better than local updates, when a dip in accuracies of local updates are observed at iterations 5 and 8, the accuracies of global updates at those iterations also spike down in a similar fashion. Similar trends of local and global accuracy trends like those observed in User 3 can also be observed in User 1 (Fig. 2a and Fig. 2d). This clearly shows that when there are lesser overlapping activity labels (User 1 and User 3), the global model does not learn the activities' characteristics much, while the global updates are more robust in spite of spikes and dips in local updates with such overlapping labels (User 2), thereby leading to higher average increase in accuracies (as observed in Table 3).

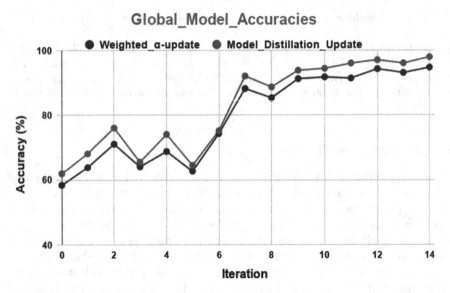

Fig. 3. Iterations vs Final Global Average Accuracies (%) with *Model Distillation Update* and *Weighted α-update*

Overall average deterministic (not relative) increase in accuracies of ~11.01% and ~9.153% are observed respectively with the model distillation and α-update versions on the HHAR dataset, which are calculated from the global model updates (Table 3). The overall global model accuracies averaged across all users after each iteration (which is different from global update accuracies after each iteration observed in Fig. 2) are also elucidated in Fig. 3. We can observe that the distillation version performs better than the α-update version with a ~3.21% deterministic accuracy increase. With our current framework, *communication (transfer) of just the model scores* of respective activity labels between clients (local devices) and the central cloud is performed, without necessitating transfer of the entire model weights, which significantly reduces latency and memory overheads.

4.2   On-Device Performance

We observe the on-device performance of our proposed framework by experimenting on a Raspberry Pi 2. We choose this single-board computing platform since it has similar hardware and software (HW/SW) specifications with that of predominant contemporary IoT/mobile devices. The computation times taken for execution of on-device federated learning and inference are reported in Table 4. This clearly shows the feasibility of our proposed system on embedded devices. Also, the distillation mechanism accounts for higher computation overheads in time on edge/mobile devices, and depend on the temperature parameters (default set at 1) and the distilled student model architecture chosen. The end-user can typically make the trade-off of choosing the local distillation version or the α-update version depending on their compute capabilities and accuracy requirements.

Table 4. Time taken for Execution

Process	Computation time
Training time per epoch in an FL iteration (i)	~1.8 s
Inference time	~16 ms
Discrete Wavelet Transform	~0.45 ms
Decimation	~4.6 ms

5   Conclusion

This paper presents a unified framework for flexibly handling heterogeneous labels and model architectures in federated learning for Human Activity Recognition (HAR). By leveraging transfer learning along with simple scenario changes in the federated learning setting, we propose a framework with two versions – *Model Distillation Update* and *Weighted α-update* aggregation in local models, and we are able to leverage the effectiveness of global model updates with activity label based averaging across all devices and obtain higher efficiencies. Moreover, overlapping activities are found to make our framework robust, and also helps in effective accuracy increase. We also experiment by sending only model scores rather than model weights from user device to server, which reduces latency and memory overheads multifold. We empirically showcase the successful feasibility of our framework on-device, for federated learning/training across different iterations on the widely used HHAR dataset. We expect a good amount of research focus hereon in handling statistical, model and label based heterogeneities for HAR and other pervasive sensing tasks.

References

1. Bonawitz, K., et al.: Towards federated learning at scale: system design. In: SysML 2019 (2019)
2. Chang, Y., Mathur, A., Isopoussu, A., Song, J., Kawsar, F.: A systematic study of unsupervised domain adaptation for robust human-activity recognition. Proc. ACM Interactive Mob. Wearable Ubiquitous Technol. **4**(1), 1–30 (2020)
3. Deng, Y., Kamani, M.M., Mahdavi, M.: Adaptive personalized federated learning. arXiv preprint arXiv:2003.13461 (2020)
4. Feng, S., Duarte, M.F.: Few-shot learning-based human activity recognition. Expert Syst. Appl. **138**, 112782 (2019)
5. Gudur, G.K., Balaji, B.S., Perepu, S.K.: Resource-constrained federated learning with heterogeneous labels and models. arXiv preprint arXiv:2011.03206 (2020)
6. Gudur, G.K., Sundaramoorthy, P., Umaashankar, V.: ActiveHARNet: towards on-device deep Bayesian active learning for human activity recognition. In: The 3rd International Workshop on Deep Learning for Mobile Systems and Applications, pp. 7–12 (2019)
7. Hammerla, N.Y., Halloran, S., Plötz, T.: Deep, convolutional, and recurrent models for human activity recognition using wearables. In: Proceedings of the Twenty-Fifth International Joint Conference on Artificial Intelligence, IJCAI 2016, pp. 1533–1540. AAAI Press (2016)
8. Hinton, G., Vinyals, O., Dean, J.: Distilling the knowledge in a neural network. In: NIPS Deep Learning and Representation Learning Workshop (2015)
9. Kairouz, P., et al.: Advances and open problems in federated learning. arXiv preprint arXiv:1912.04977 (2019)
10. Kingma, D.P., Ba, J.: Adam: A method for stochastic optimization. arXiv preprint arXiv:1412.6980 (2014)
11. Konečný, J., McMahan, H.B., Ramage, D., Richtárik, P.: Federated optimization: Distributed machine learning for on-device intelligence. arXiv preprint arXiv:1610.02527 (2016)
12. Lane, N.D., Bhattacharya, S., Georgiev, P., Forlivesi, C., Kawsar, F.: An early resource characterization of deep learning on wearables, smartphones and internet-of-things devices. In: Proceedings of the 2015 International Workshop on Internet of Things Towards Applications, pp. 7–12. IoT-App 2015 (2015)
13. Li, D., Wang, J.: FedMD: heterogenous federated learning via model distillation. arXiv preprint arXiv:1910.03581 (2019)
14. Li, T., Sahu, A.K., Talwalkar, A., Smith, V.: Federated learning: challenges, methods, and future directions. IEEE Sig. Process. Mag. **37**, 50–60 (2020)
15. Li, T., Sahu, A.K., Zaheer, M., Sanjabi, M., Talwalkar, A., Smith, V.: Federated optimization in heterogeneous networks. Proc. Mach. Learn. Syst. **2020**, 429–450 (2020)
16. Lim, W.Y.B., et al.: Federated learning in mobile edge networks: a comprehensive survey. IEEE Commun. Surv. Tutorials (2020)
17. McMahan, H.B., Moore, E., Ramage, D., Hampson, S., Arcas, B.A.Y.: Communication-efficient learning of deep networks from decentralized data. In: Proceedings of the 20th International Conference on Artificial Intelligence and Statistics, vol. 54, pp. 1273–1282 (2017)
18. Osmani, V., Balasubramaniam, S., Botvich, D.: Human activity recognition in pervasive health-care: supporting efficient remote collaboration. J. Netw. Comput. Appl. **31**, 628–655 (2008)

19. Ramakrishnan, A.K., Naqvi, N.Z., Preuveneers, D., Berbers, Y.: Federated mobile activity recognition using a smart service adapter for cloud offloading. In: Park, J., Jin, Q., Sang-soo Yeo, M., Hu, B. (eds.) Human Centric Technology and Service in Smart Space, pp. 173–180. Springer, Heidelberg (2012). https://doi.org/10.1007/978-94-007-5086-9_23

20. Sozinov, K., Vlassov, V., Girdzijauskas, S.: Human activity recognition using federated learning. In: 2018 IEEE International Conference on Parallel & Distributed Processing with Applications, Ubiquitous Computing & Communications, Big Data & Cloud Computing, Social Computing & Networking, Sustainable Computing & Communications (ISPA/IUCC/BDCloud/SocialCom/SustainCom), pp. 1103–1111. IEEE (2018)

21. Stisen, A., et al.: Smart devices are different: assessing and mitigating mobile sensing heterogeneities for activity recognition. In: Proceedings of the 13th ACM Conference on Embedded Networked Sensor Systems, SenSys 2015, pp. 127–140 (2015)

22. Sundaramoorthy, P., Gudur, G.K., Moorthy, M.R., Bhandari, R.N., Vijayaraghavan, V.: HARNet: towards on-device incremental learning using deep ensembles on constrained devices. In: Proceedings of the 2nd International Workshop on Embedded and Mobile Deep Learning, pp. 31–36. EMDL 2018 (2018)

23. Yao, S., Hu, S., Zhao, Y., Zhang, A., Abdelzaher, T.: Deepsense: a unified deep learning framework for time-series mobile sensing data processing. In: Proceedings of the 26th International Conference on World Wide Web, WWW 2017, pp. 351–360 (2017)

24. Yao, S., Zhao, Y., Shao, H., Zhang, C., Zhang, A., Hu, S., Liu, D., Liu, S., Su, L., Abdelzaher, T.: SenseGAN: enabling deep learning for internet of things with a semi-supervised framework. Proc. ACM Interactive Mob. Wearable Ubiquitous Technol. 2(3), 1–21 (2018)

25. Zhao, Y., Li, M., Lai, L., Suda, N., Civin, D., Chandra, V.: Federated learning with non-iid data. arXiv preprint arXiv:1806.00582 (2018)

ARID: A New Dataset for Recognizing Action in the Dark

Yuecong Xu[1], Jianfei Yang[1(✉)], Haozhi Cao[1], Kezhi Mao[1],
Jianxiong Yin[2], and Simon See[2]

[1] School of Electrical and Electronic Engineering, Nanyang Technological University,
Singapore, Singapore
{xuyu0014,yang0478,haozhi001,ekzmao}@ntu.edu.sg
[2] NVIDIA AI Tech Centre, Singapore, Singapore
{jianxiongy,ssee}@nvidia.com

Abstract. The task of action recognition in dark videos is useful in various scenarios, e.g., night surveillance and self-driving at night. Though progress has been made in action recognition task for videos in normal illumination, few have studied action recognition in the dark, partly due to the lack of sufficient datasets for such a task. In this paper, we explored the task of action recognition in dark videos. We bridge the gap of the lack of data by collecting a new dataset: the Action Recognition in the Dark (ARID) dataset. It consists of 3,784 video clips with 11 action categories. To the best of our knowledge, it is the first dataset focused on human actions in dark videos. To gain further understanding of our ARID dataset, we analyze our dataset in detail and showed its necessity over synthetic dark videos. Additionally, we benchmark the performance of current action recognition models on our dataset and explored potential methods for increasing their performances. We show that current action recognition models and frame enhancement methods may not be effective solutions for the task of action recognition in dark videos (data available at https://xuyu0010.github.io/arid).

Keywords: Action recognition · Dark videos · Convolution neural network · Benchmark

1 Introduction

Thanks to the increasing application of automatic action recognition in various fields, such as surveillance [24] and smart homes [20], action recognition tasks have received considerable attention in recent years. Although much progress has been made, current research mostly focused on videos shot under normal illumination. This is partly because current datasets for action recognition are normally collected from web videos shot mostly under normal illumination. Yet videos shot in the dark are useful in many cases, such as night surveillance, and self-driving at night. Additional sensors, such as infrared or thermal imaging sensors, could be utilized for recognizing actions in the dark. However, such

© Springer Nature Singapore Pte Ltd. 2021
X. Li et al. (Eds.): DL-HAR 2020, CCIS 1370, pp. 70–84, 2021.
https://doi.org/10.1007/978-981-16-0575-8_6

sensors are of high cost and cannot be deployed on a large scale. Hence we focus on action recognition in the dark without additional sensors. To this end, we collected a new dataset: Action Recognition In the Dark (ARID) dataset, dedicated to the task of action recognition in dark videos. To the best of our knowledge, it is the first dataset focusing on human actions in the dark.

Currently, there already exist a large number of videos in various datasets, shot under normal illumination. It is intuitive to make use of these videos by creating synthetic dark videos based on them. In this paper, we prove the necessity of a dataset with real dark videos through a detailed analysis and comparison with synthetic dark videos. We observe distinct characteristics of real dark videos that cannot be replicated by synthetic dark videos.

Recently, neural networks, especially the convolutional neural network (CNN) based solutions have proven to be effective for various computer vision tasks. For action recognition, state-of-the-art results on previous action recognition datasets are mostly achieved through 3D-CNN based networks. To gain further understanding of the challenges faced with action recognition in dark videos, we analyze how dark videos affect current action recognition models. Additionally, we explore potential solutions for substantial improvements in action recognition accuracy utilizing current models.

In summary, we explored the task of action recognition in dark videos. The contribution of this work is threefold: 1) we propose a new ARID dataset, dedicated to the task of recognizing actions in dark videos; 2) we verify the importance of our ARID dataset through statistical and visual analysis and comparison with synthetic dark videos; 3) we benchmark the performance of current 3D-CNN based action recognition models on our dataset while exploring potential methods to improve accuracy with current models, and reveals challenges in the task of action recognition in dark videos.

2   Related Works

Action Recognition Datasets. There are several benchmark datasets in the action recognition domain. Earlier datasets, such as KTH [14] and Weizmann [4], contain relatively small number of action classes. With the rapidly increased performance of proposed methods on these smaller datasets, larger and more challenging datasets are introduced. This includes HMDB51 [10], UCF101 [15] and Kinetics [1]. Particularly, the Kinetics dataset, with 400 action classes and more than 160,000 clips in total, becomes the primary choice. Though these datasets involve an abundant scale of actions, these actions are mostly collected from web videos, mostly recorded under normal illumination. Hence, to study the action recognition performance in dark videos, we collected a new video dataset dedicated to videos shot in the dark.

Dark Visual Datasets. Recently, there has been a rise of research interest with regards to computer vision tasks in the dark environment, such as face recognition in the dark. The research for dark environment visual tasks is partly supported by the various dark visual datasets introduced. Among these, most datasets focused on image enhancement and denoising tasks, where the goal is to visually enhance dark images for a clearer view. These include LOL Dataset [19] and SID [3]. More recently, such an enhancement task has been expanded to the video domain. New datasets include DRV [2] and SMOID [8]. Although both datasets contain dark videos, their focus is more towards enhancing the visibility of video frames. The scenes are randomly shot and may not include specific human actions. In contrast, our ARID dataset focuses on classifying different human actions in dark videos.

3   Action Recognition in the Dark Dataset

Although a small amount of videos taken in the dark do exist in current action recognition datasets, such as Kinetics and HMDB51, the task of human action recognition in dark environment has rarely been studied. This is partly due to the very low proportion of dark videos in current benchmark datasets, and a lack of datasets dedicated to action analysis in the dark. To bridge the gap in the lack of dark video data, we introduce a new Action Recognition In the Dark (ARID) dataset. In this session, we take an overview of the dataset in three perspectives: the action classes, the process of data collection as well as some basic statistics of our ARID dataset.

Action Classes. The ARID dataset includes a total of 11 common human action classes. The list of action classes can be categorized into two types: *Singular Person Actions*, which includes jumping, running, turning, walking and waving; and *Person Actions with Objects*, which includes drinking, picking, pouring, pushing, sitting and standing. Figure 1 shows the sample frames for each of the 11 action classes in the ARID dataset.

Fig. 1. Sample frames for each of the 11 action classes of the ARID dataset. All samples are manually tuned brighter for display purposes. Best viewed in color and zoomed in. (Color figure online)

Data Collection. The video clips in the ARID dataset are collected using 3 different commercial cameras. The clips are shot strictly during night hours. All clips are collected from a total of 11 volunteers, among which 8 males and 3 females. We collected the clips in 9 outdoor scenes and 9 indoor scenes, such as carparks, corridors and playing fields for outdoor scenes, and classrooms and laboratories for indoor scenes. The lighting condition of each scene is different, with no direct light shot on the actor in almost all videos. In many cases, it is challenging even for the naked eye to recognize the human action without tuning the raw video clips.

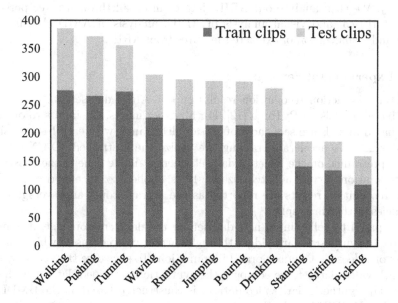

Fig. 2. The distribution of clips among all action classes in ARID. The dark grey and light grey bars indicate the number of clips in the train and test partitions.

Basic Statistics. The ARID dataset contains a total of 3,784 video clips, with each class containing at least 110 clips. The clips of a single action class are divided into 12–18 groups with each group containing no less than 7 clips. The clips in the same group share some similar features, such as being shot under similar lighting conditions or shot with the same actor. Figure 2 shows the number of distribution of clips among all the classes. The training and testing sets are partitioned by splitting the clip groups, with a ratio of 7:3. We selected three train/test splits, such that each group would have an equal chance to be present in either the train partition or the test partition.

The video clips are fixed to a frame rate of 30 FPS with a resolution of 320×240. The minimum clip length is 1.2 s with 36 frames, and the duration of the whole dataset is 8,721 s. The videos are saved in .avi format and are compressed using the *DivX* codec.

4   Experiments and Discussions

In this section, we gain further understanding of our proposed dataset through a detailed analysis of the ARID dataset. The main objectives are twofold: 1) validate the necessity of a video dataset collected in the real dark environment and 2) provide a benchmark for current action recognition datasets while revealing the challenges with regards to the task of action recognition in dark videos. In the following, we first introduce the experiment settings along with the construction of a synthetic dark video dataset. We then introduce methods used to enhance dark video frames in ARID in an effort to improve action recognition accuracy. We then analyze our ARID dataset in detail through three perspectives: statistical and visual analysis of ARID, analysis of ARID classification result and visualization of extracted features from ARID.

4.1   Experimental Settings

To obtain the action recognition results on our ARID dataset, we utilize 3D-CNN based models on PyTorch [12]. For all experiments, the inputs to our 3D-CNN based models are sequences of 16 sampled frames with each frame resized to 224×224. To accelerate training, we utilize the pretrained 3D-CNN based models pretrained on the Kinetics dataset when available. Due to the constraint in computation power, a batch size of 16 is applied to all experiments. The action recognition results are reported as the average top-1 and average top-5 accuracies of the three splits.

Compared to collecting a new dataset for the dark environment, it is more intuitive to synthesize dark videos through current video datasets which mainly consist of videos shot under normal illumination. To showcase the necessity of a real dark video dataset, we compare the synthetic dark video dataset with our ARID. The synthetic dark video dataset is constructed based on the HMDB51, denoted as HMDB51-dark. We synthesize dark videos by gamma intensity correction formulated as:

$$D(t, x, y) = I(t, x, y)^{(1/\gamma)} \tag{1}$$

where $D(t, x, y)$ is the value of the pixel in the synthetic dark video, located at spatial location (x, y) at the tth frame, and $I(t, x, y)$ is the pixel value of the corresponding pixel in the original video. Both $D(t, x, y)$ and $I(t, x, y)$ are in the range of $[0, 1]$. γ is the parameter that controls the degree of darkness in the synthetic dark video, typically in the range of $[0.1, 10]$, where a smaller number would result in lower pixel values, producing darker synthetic videos.

We note that the dark videos collected in our ARID are shot under different illumination conditions. To mimic the differences in illumination, we apply different γ values when synthesizing dark videos. More specifically, the γ value is obtained randomly from a normal distribution $\mathcal{N}(\mu, \sigma^2)$ with the constraint of $\gamma \geq 0.1$. Here the mean μ is set to 0.2 and the standard deviation σ is set to 0.07. Figure 3 shows the comparison of sample frames of videos from the original HMDB51 dataset with the sample frames from the corresponding synthetic dark videos.

Fig. 3. Comparison of a sample frame of normal illumination taken from the video in the HMDB51 dataset (left) and the corresponding frame taken from the synthetic dark video from our HMDB51-dark dataset (right). The frame in the original HMDB51 video has more details, including the background and a clearer contour of the actor. Best viewed in color. (Color figure online)

4.2 Frame Enhancement Methods

For humans to better recognize actions in dark videos, an intuitive method is to enhance each dark video frame. In this paper, we investigate the effect of applying different frame enhancement methods on ARID towards current action recognition models. We applied five frame enhancement methods: Histogram Equalization (**HE**) [16], Gamma Intensity Correction (**GIC**), **LIME** [5], **BIMEF** [21] and **KinD** [22]. Among them, **HE** and **GIC** are traditional image enhancement methods. **HE** produces higher contrast images, whereas **GIC** is used to adjust the luminance of images. Both **LIME** and **BIMEF** are based on the Retinex theory [11], which assumes that images are composed of reflection and illumination. **LIME** estimates the illumination map of dark images while imposing a structure prior to the initial illumination map, while **BIMEF** proposes a multi-exposure fusion algorithm. **KinD** is a deep neural network-based method utilizing a two-stream structure for reflectance restoration and illumination adjustment. The KinD is implemented with weights pretrained on the LOL Dataset. The result of applying the above methods to the ARID dataset are denoted as ARID-HE, ARID-GIC, ARID-LIME, ARID-BIMEF, and ARID-KinD respectively. The **GIC** is also applied to the synthetic dark dataset HMDB51-dark, whose result is denoted as HMDB51-dark-GIC.

4.3 Statistical and Visual Analysis of ARID

To better understand real dark videos and understand the necessity of real dark videos, we compute and compare the statistics of the ARID dataset with the HMDB51 dataset as well as the synthetic HMDB51-dark dataset. Table 1 presents the detailed mean value and standard deviation value of datasets ARID, ARID-GIC, HMDB51, HMDB51-dark and HMDB51-dark-GIC respectively. The gamma values γ for both ARID-GIC and HMDB51-dark-GIC are both set to 5.

The mean and standard deviation values of ARID as shown in Table 1 depict the characteristics of videos in our ARID dataset. Compared to the original HMDB51, the RGB mean and standard deviation values of the ARID dataset are both lower than that of the HMDB51 dataset. This indicates that video

Table 1. RGB mean and standard deviation values of various datasets, including ARID and its **GIC** enhanced output ARID-GIC, HMDB51 and the synthetic dark dataset HMDB51-dark, as well as the **GIC** enhanced output of the synthetic dart dataset, HMDB51-dark-GIC. All values are normalized to the range of [0.0. 1.0].

Dataset	RGB mean values	RGB standard deviations
ARID	[0.0796, 0.0739, 0.0725]	[0.1005, 0.0971, 0.0899]
ARID-GIC	[0.5473, 0.5418, 0.5391]	[0.1101, 0.1102, 0.1022]
HMDB51	[0.4248, 0.4082, 0.3676]	[0.2695, 0.2724, 0.2779]
HMDB51-dark	[0.0979, 0.0884, 0.0818]	[0.1836, 0.1840, 0.1789]
HMDB51-dark-GIC	[0.4904, 0.4816, 0.4588]	[0.3593, 0.3600, 0.3486]

frames in ARID are lower in brightness and contrast compared to video frames in HMDB51. This is further justified by the sampled frames and their RGB and Y histograms comparison between ARID and HMDB51 datasets, as shown in Fig. 4(a) and (c). The lower brightness and lower contrast for video frames in ARID make it challenging even for the human naked eye to identify the actions.

We observe that our real dark dataset ARID and the synthetic dark dataset HMDB51-dark are very similar in terms of the RGB mean values. This in part, shows that our synthesized operation mimics the real dark environment well. However, further comparison in terms of RGB standard deviation values indicates that the real dark dataset ARID is still lower in contrast. This matches the observation of comparison between the sampled frames of ARID and HMDB51-dark, as shown in Fig. 4(a) and (d). Here we observe that videos from HMDB51-dark would visually be more distinguishable. We argue that this is due to the fact that bright pixels in the original HMDB51 dataset, whose corresponding output pixels in the synthetic dark videos have higher pixel values. This raises both the standard deviation of HMDB51-dark, which in terms is reflected as frames with higher contrast.

As mentioned in Sect. 4.2, the **GIC** method could enhance frames by adjusting the luminance of the frames. By setting $\gamma \geq 1.0$, the resulting pixel value after applying the **GIC** method should be larger than the input pixel value. This is justified by the larger RGB mean values of ARID-GIC and HMDB51-dark-GIC compared to ARID and HMDB51-dark datasets. Sampled frames as shown in Fig. 4(a) and (b) also justifies that **GIC** enhancement greatly increases the visibility of each video frame. The person seen running can not be clearly observed by the naked eye in Fig. 4(a), whereas the person becomes more visible in Fig. 4(b).

Though the comparison of sampled frames across Fig. 4(a)(b) and (d)(e) shows the effectiveness of **GIC** enhancement in increasing luminance of dark videos, there is still a significant difference between ARID-GIC and HMDB51-dark-GIC. The most significant difference is that standard deviation of ARID-GIC is much smaller than that of HMDB51-dark-GIC. This indicates that videos

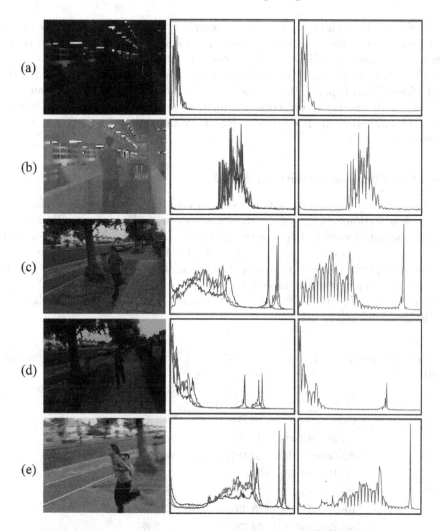

Fig. 4. Comparison of sampled frames and the RGB (middle column) and Y (right column) value histograms of their corresponding videos from (a) ARID, (b) ARID-GIC, (c) HMDB51, (d) HMDB51-dark and (d) HMDB51-dark-GIC datasets. **GIC** enhancement shifts the RGB and Y value histograms towards the larger values, indicating brighter video frames. The RGB and Y values of ARID and ARID-GIC are more concentrated than that of HMDB51-dark and HMDB51-dark-GIC respectively, which matches the low contrast and pale sampled images. The peaks of the RGB histogram at the higher values of the HMDB51-dark video comes from the bright background. Best viewed in color and zoomed in. (Color figure online)

in ARID-GIC are still low in contrast after the **GIC** enhancement. This is justified by comparing the sampled frames as shown in Fig. 4(b) and (e), where we observe that the sampled frame from ARID-GIC looks pale as compared to that from HMDB51-dark-GIC.

From the above observation, we can summarize the main characteristic of the real dark videos collected in our ARID dataset: low brightness and low contrast. Though the character of low brightness could be mimicked by the synthetic dark videos, the characteristic of low contrast cannot be easily mimicked by synthetic dark videos. This is partly due to the bright backgrounds and pixels commonly existing in videos shot under normal illumination. The above analysis confirms that real dark videos are irreplaceable for the task of action recognition in a dark environment.

4.4   Classification Results on ARID

In this section, we illustrate how current action recognition models perform in the task of action recognition in the dark on our ARID dataset. We further explore potential ways to improve the performance of action recognition in real dark videos, and reveal some challenges faced with action recognition in dark videos. The performance of current competitive 3D-CNN-based action recognition models are presented in Table 2, which includes: C3D [17], 3D-ShuffleNet [9], 3D-SqueezeNet [7], 3D-ResNet-18 [18], Pseudo-3D-199 [13], Res50-I3D [1] and 3D-ResNext-101 [6].

Table 2. Performance of current 3D-CNN-based action recognition models on the ARID dataset.

Method	Top-1 accuracy	Top-5 accuracy
C3D	39.17%	94.17%
3D-ShuffleNet	44.35%	93.44%
3D-SqueezeNet	50.18%	94.17%
3D-ResNet-18	54.68%	96.60%
Pseudo-3D-199	71.93%	98.66%
Res50-I3D	73.39%	97.21%
3D-ResNext-101	74.73%	98.54%

The performance results as shown in Table 2 show that among the current action recognition models, 3D-ResNext-101 performs the best with a top-1 accuracy of 74.73%. We notice that the top-5 accuracy is relatively high for all methods, which is partly because of the small number of classes in our dataset.

We also notice that though our dataset is of relatively small size and has fewer classes than current normal illumination video datasets, there is plenty of room for improvement in accuracy. To explore potential ways for further improving accuracy for dark videos, we choose 3D-ResNext-101 as the baseline for experiments. An intuitive method for improving accuracy is the use of frame enhancement methods as introduced in Sect. 4.2. To test whether frame enhancement methods could improve accuracy, we employ **GIC** method on the synthetic HMDB51-dark dataset due to its larger data size and ease of obtaining dark data from the current datasets. The performance of 3D-ResNext-101 on the synthetic dataset HMDB51-dark and its corresponding **GIC** enhanced HMDB51-dark-GIC is illustrated in Table 3.

Table 3. Performance of 3D-ResNext-101 on the synthetic HMDB51-dark and its **GIC** enhanced HMDB51-dark-GIC. The performance of 3D-ResNext-101 on the original HMDB51 is presented for reference.

Dataset	Top-1 accuracy
HMDB51-dark	44.90%
HMDB51-dark-GIC	56.62%
HMDB51	63.80%

The results as presented in Table 3 show a sharp decrease in classification accuracy when the same network is utilized for the dark data. The decrease is expected, given that dark videos contain fewer details as shown in Fig. 3. Besides this, we also notice a significant increase of 11.72% in accuracy when the **GIC** method is applied to enhance the dark video frames. As the synthetic data is darkened with random gamma values while the **GIC** enhancement utilizes a fixed gamma value, it is nearly impossible to recover the original videos. Despite this, the **GIC** operation still brings a significant amount of accuracy improvement.

The success in applying frame enhancement methods for increasing classification accuracy in synthetic dark videos give us a hint on potential ways to improve accuracy for action recognition in real dark videos. To justify if the same **GIC** method could also improve action recognition accuracy on our ARID dataset, we perform experiments on the **GIC** enhanced ARID dataset: ARID-GIC, utilizing 3D-ResNext-101. The result is as presented in Table 4.

Table 4. Performance of 3D-ResNext-101 on variants of ARID enhanced by **HE**, **GIC**, **LIME**, **BIMEF** and **KinD**. The Improvement is compared with the performance of 3D-ResNext-101 on the original ARID dataset.

Dataset	Top-1 accuracy	Improvement
ARID-GIC	78.03%	3.30%
ARID-HE	75.82%	1.09%
ARID-LIME	77.40%	2.67%
ARID-BIMEF	73.39%	−1.34%
ARID-KinD	69.62%	−5.11%
ARID	74.73%	/

The results in Table 4 illustrate that the action recognition accuracy of our ARID would improve through **GIC** enhancement, thanks to the increase in the illumination of each video frame as presented in Fig. 4. The increase in accuracy is consistent with the findings with regards to the synthetic dark dataset HMDB51-dark. However, we also notice that the improvement of performance by using **GIC** is only 3.3%, which is rather limited compared to the improvement in the synthetic dark dataset. As **GIC** method is a method based on simple exponential calculation, we further examine if more sophisticated frame enhancement methods could further improve action recognition accuracy. We thus examine the accuracy on datasets ARID-HE, ARID-LIME, ARID-BIMEF and ARID-KinD, which are results of the output by frame enhancement methods **HE**, **LIME**, **BIMEF** and **KinD** respectively. The results are also presented in Table 4.

Interestingly, Table 4 illustrates that not all frame enhancement methods result in improvements in action recognition accuracy in dark videos. Of all the frame enhancement methods, the largest improvement is achieved by the **GIC** method. Whereas the accuracy drops the most utilizing the recent deep learning-based method **KinD**. To gain a better understanding of the differences between the outcome of utilizing the different enhancement methods, we visualize the frame output of each enhancement method. Figure 5 presents the sampled frames of the output of the above enhancement methods with the same input ARID video frame.

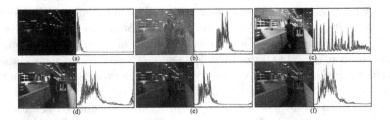

Fig. 5. Comparison of the sampled frames and their RGB histograms from (a) ARID, (b) ARID-GIC, (c) ARID-HE, (d) ARID-LIME, (e) ARID-BIMEF and (f) ARID-KinD.

Figure 5 clearly shows that visually, the outputs of all frame enhancement methods improve the visibility of the video. The actor who is running can be seen clearly in all sampled frames except the sample frame from the original video in ARID. However, the sampled frame of ARID-GIC does not appear to be the best enhancement visually, as it is still low in contrast. In comparison, all other methods produce higher contrast images, as justified by the RGB histograms in Fig. 5. This indicates that current frame enhancement which clearly improves dark video frames visually may not bring improvement in action recognition accuracy for dark videos. We argue that some enhancement can be regarded as artifact or adversarial attack for videos. Though enhanced frames are clearer visually, some enhancements break the original distribution of videos and introduce noise. The change in distribution and introduction of noise could lead to a decrease in performance for action recognition models.

4.5   Feature Visualization with ARID

To further understand the performance of current action recognition models on ARID and analyze the effect of dark videos on current models, we extract and visualize features at the last convolution layer using 3D-ResNext-101. The visualization of features are presented as *Class Activation Maps (CAM)* [23], which depicts the focus of the model with respect to the given prediction. Figure 6 and Fig. 7 compare the sampled frames from the ARID and HMDB51 datasets, with the corresponding *CAM*s. We observe that for the frames in HMDB51 with normal illumination as shown in Fig. 6, the 3D-ResNext-101 model is able to focus on the actors, whereas for the dark video, the model focuses more on the background. For example, for the action shown in Fig. 7(a)(left), the network classifies the action as action "Jumping" by focusing on the background whose details are uncovered due to the person jumping backward. Therefore the *CAM* shows that the network focuses on a narrow beam in the background. The focus on the background instead of the actor could be partly due to the fact that clear outlines of actors rarely exist in dark videos.

Fig. 6. *CAM*s of sampled frames from 3 classes of HMDB51: Jumping (left), Running (mid) and Standing (right).

In Table 4, certain frame enhancement methods could positively affect the final classification accuracy. To gain further understanding of how the different frame enhancement methods actually affect the action recognition models, we compare the *CAM*s with respect to the same sampled frame from the five frame enhanced ARID datasets as shown in Fig. 7. Compared with the original video frame, the outline of the actor is much clearer in all enhanced frames. We observe that the focus area of the network is more concentrated compared with *CAM* of the original frame. Additionally, we observe some offset between the focus of the network of the frame enhanced sample frames and the actual actor. In comparison, the *CAM*s of HMDB51 video frames show the network focuses center around the actors. This may partly explain the inability of frame enhancement methods to improve action recognition accuracy while being able to focus on a more concentrated area of each video frame.

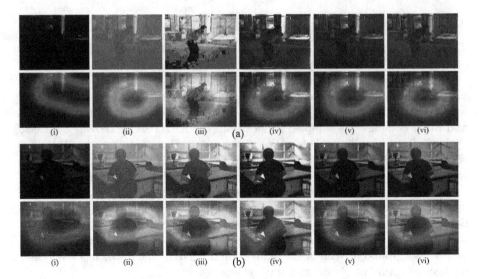

Fig. 7. Comparison of sampled frames and their corresponding *CAM*s of classes: (a) Jumping and (b) Standing. The sampled frames and their *CAM*s are from (i) ARID, (ii) ARID-GIC, (iii) ARID-HE, (iv) ARID-LIME, (v) ARID-BIMEF and (vi) ARID-KinD.

4.6 Discussion

From the results and analysis presented above, we can draw three major conclusions about the task of action recognition in the dark. First, videos taken in a dark environment are characterized by its low brightness and low contrast. As the characteristic of low contrast cannot be fully synthesized, synthetic dark videos cannot be directly applied to action recognition in the dark. Second, though current frame enhancement methods could produce visually clearer video frames, the accuracy improvements made for current action recognition models after frame enhancing dark videos is rather limited. Some frame enhancement methods even deteriorate classification accuracy, since some enhancement can be regarded as artifact or adversarial attack for videos. Breaking the original distribution of videos might decrease the performance of a statistical model. Better frame enhancement methods developed may be helpful in improving action recognition accuracy in dark videos. Third, in many dark videos, current action recognition models fail to focus on the actor for classification. This might be caused by unclear outlines of actors and shows that action recognition models could tend to focus on the actors for frame enhanced dark videos. However, the focus in frame enhanced dark videos contain offsets. We believe that better action recognition models with a better ability to focus on actors, especially with unclear outlines, could be a critical part of improving action recognition accuracy in dark videos. These conclusions contribute to exploring more effective solutions for ARID.

5 Conclusion

In this work, we introduced the Action Recognition In the Dark (ARID) dataset, which is, as far as we are aware, the first dataset dedicated to the task of action recognition in the dark. The ARID includes 4k video clips with 11 action categories. To understand the challenges behind real dark videos, we analyze our ARID dataset with three perspectives: statistical, classification result, and feature visualization. We discover distinct characteristics of real dark videos that are different from synthetic dark videos. Our analysis shows that current action recognition models and frame enhancement methods are not effective enough in recognizing action in dark videos. We hope this study could draw more interest to work on the task of action recognition in the dark.

References

1. Carreira, J., Zisserman, A.: Quo vadis, action recognition? A new model and the kinetics dataset. In: Proceedings of the IEEE Conference on Computer Vision and Pattern Recognitionm, pp. 6299–6308 (2017)
2. Chen, C., Chen, Q., Do, M.N., Koltun, V.: Seeing motion in the dark. In: Proceedings of the IEEE International Conference on Computer Vision, pp. 3185–3194 (2019)
3. Chen, C., Chen, Q., Xu, J., Koltun, V.: Learning to see in the dark. In: Proceedings of the IEEE Conference on Computer Vision and Pattern Recognition, pp. 3291–3300 (2018)
4. Gorelick, L., Blank, M., Shechtman, E., Irani, M., Basri, R.: Actions as space-time shapes. IEEE Trans. Pattern Anal. Mach. Intell. **29**(12), 2247–2253 (2007)
5. Guo, X., Li, Y., Ling, H.: Lime: Low-light image enhancement via illumination map estimation. IEEE Trans. Image Process. **26**(2), 982–993 (2016)
6. Hara, K., Kataoka, H., Satoh, Y.: Can spatiotemporal 3D CNNS retrace the history of 2D CNNS and imagenet? In: Proceedings of the IEEE Conference on Computer Vision and Pattern Recognition, pp. 6546–6555 (2018)
7. Iandola, F.N., Han, S., Moskewicz, M.W., Ashraf, K., Dally, W.J., Keutzer, K.: SqueezeNet: alexnet-level accuracy with 50x fewer parameters and <0.5 MB model size. arXiv preprint arXiv:1602.07360 (2016)
8. Jiang, H., Zheng, Y.: Learning to see moving objects in the dark. In: Proceedings of the IEEE International Conference on Computer Vision, pp. 7324–7333 (2019)
9. Köpüklü, O., Kose, N., Gunduz, A., Rigoll, G.: Resource efficient 3D convolutional neural networks. arXiv preprint arXiv:1904.02422 (2019)
10. Kuehne, H., Jhuang, H., Garrote, E., Poggio, T., Serre, T.: HMDB: a large video database for human motion recognition. In: 2011 International Conference on Computer Vision, pp. 2556–2563. IEEE (2011)
11. Land, E.H.: The retinex theory of color vision. Sci. Am. **237**(6), 108–129 (1977)
12. Paszke, A., et al.: Automatic differentiation in PyTorch. In: NIPS Autodiff Workshop (2017)
13. Qiu, Z., Yao, T., Mei, T.: Learning spatio-temporal representation with pseudo-3D residual networks. In: Proceedings of the IEEE International Conference on Computer Vision, pp. 5533–5541 (2017)

14. Schuldt, C., Laptev, I., Caputo, B.: Recognizing human actions: a local SVM approach. In: Proceedings of the 17th International Conference on Pattern Recognition, ICPR 2004. vol. 3, pp. 32–36. IEEE (2004)
15. Soomro, K., Zamir, A.R., Shah, M.: UCF101: a dataset of 101 human actions classes from videos in the wild. arXiv preprint arXiv:1212.0402 (2012)
16. Trahanias, P., Venetsanopoulos, A.: Color image enhancement through 3-D histogram equalization. In: Proceedings, 11th IAPR International Conference on Pattern Recognition. vol. III. Conference C: Image, Speech and Signal Analysis, pp. 545–548. IEEE (1992)
17. Tran, D., Bourdev, L., Fergus, R., Torresani, L., Paluri, M.: Learning spatiotemporal features with 3d convolutional networks. In: Proceedings of the IEEE International Conference on Computer Vision, pp. 4489–4497 (2015)
18. Tran, D., Wang, H., Torresani, L., Ray, J., LeCun, Y., Paluri, M.: A closer look at spatiotemporal convolutions for action recognition. In: Proceedings of the IEEE conference on Computer Vision and Pattern Recognition, pp. 6450–6459 (2018)
19. Wei, C., Chen, W., Yang, W., Liu, J.: Deep retinex decomposition for low-light enhancement. In: British Machine Vision Conference. British Machine Vision Association (2018)
20. Yang, J., Zou, H., Jiang, H., Xie, L.: Device-free occupant activity sensing using WIFI-enabled IoT devices for smart homes. IEEE Internet Things J. 5(5), 3991–4002 (2018)
21. Ying, Z., Li, G., Ren, Y., Wang, R., Wang, W.: A new image contrast enhancement algorithm using exposure fusion framework. In: Felsberg, M., Heyden, A., Krüger, N. (eds.) CAIP 2017. LNCS, vol. 10425, pp. 36–46. Springer, Cham (2017). https://doi.org/10.1007/978-3-319-64698-5_4
22. Zhang, Y., Zhang, J., Guo, X.: Kindling the darkness: a practical low-light image enhancer. In: Proceedings of the 27th ACM International Conference on Multimedia, MM 2019, pp. 1632–1640. ACM, New York (2019). https://doi.org/10.1145/3343031.3350926
23. Zhou, B., Khosla, A., Lapedriza, A., Oliva, A., Torralba, A.: Learning deep features for discriminative localization. In: Computer Vision and Pattern Recognition (2016)
24. Zou, H., Yang, J., Prasanna Das, H., Liu, H., Zhou, Y., Spanos, C.J.: WiFi and vision multimodal learning for accurate and robust device-free human activity recognition. In: Proceedings of the IEEE Conference on Computer Vision and Pattern Recognition Workshops (2019)

Single Run Action Detector over Video Stream - A Privacy Preserving Approach

Anbumalar Saravanan[1], Justin Sanchez[1(✉)], Hassan Ghasemzadeh[2],
Aurelia Macabasco-O'Connell[3], and Hamed Tabkhi[1]

[1] University of North Carolina at Charlotte, Charlotte, NC 28223, USA
{asaravan,jsanch19,htabkhiv}@uncc.edu
[2] Washington State University, Pullman, WA 99164, USA
hassan.ghasemzadeh@wsu.edu
[3] Azusa Pacific University, Azusa, CA 91702, USA
amacabascooconnell@apu.edu

Abstract. This paper takes initial strides at designing and evaluating a vision-based system for privacy ensured activity monitoring. The proposed technology utilizing Artificial Intelligence (AI)-empowered proactive systems offering continuous monitoring, behavioral analysis, and modeling of human activities. To this end, this paper presents Single Run Action Detector (S-RAD) which is a real-time privacy-preserving action detector that performs end-to-end action localization and classification. It is based on Faster-RCNN combined with temporal shift modeling and segment based sampling to capture the human actions. Results on UCF-Sports and UR Fall dataset present comparable accuracy to State-of-the-Art approaches with significantly lower model size and computation demand and the ability for real-time execution on edge embedded device (e.g. Nvidia Jetson Xavier).

Keywords: Action detection · Deep learning · Real time · Edge computing · Spatial-temporal neural network

1 Introduction

In recent years, deep learning has achieved success in fields such as computer vision and natural language processing. Compared to traditional machine learning methods such as support vector and random forest, deep learning has a strong learning ability from the data and can make better use of datasets for feature extraction. Because of this practicability, deep learning had become more and more popular to do research works.

Deep learning models usually adopt hierarchical structures to connect their layers. The output of a lower layer can be regarded as the input of a higher layer using linear or nonlinear functions. These models can transform low-level features to high-level abstract features from the input data. Because of this characteristic, deep learning models are stronger than shallow machine learning models in feature representation. The performance of traditional machine-learning methods

X. Li et al. (Eds.): DL-HAR 2020, CCIS 1370, pp. 85–98, 2021.
https://doi.org/10.1007/978-981-16-0575-8_7

usually rely on user experiences and handcrafted methods, while deep learning approaches rely on the data.

The recent approaches in video analytic and deep learning algorithms like Convolutional Neural network provides the opportunity for real-time detection and analysis of human behaviors like walking, running or sitting down, which are part of daily living Activities (ADL) [18]. Cameras provide very rich information about persons and environments and their presence is becoming more important in everyday environments like airports, train and bus stations, malls, elderly care and even streets. Therefore, reliable vision-based action detection systems is required for various application like healthcare assistance system, crime detection and sports monitoring system. In our paper we explored two different domains (Sport and Healthcare), to prove the comprehensive nature of our proposed action detector algorithm. Approaches like [1,3,5,9] use larger CNN models that impose huge computation demand and thus limit their application in real-time constrained systems, in particular on embedded edge devices. Additionally, these methods have not been designed to fulfill requirements of pervasive video systems including privacy-preserving and real-time responsiveness. Other works done in this area are based on the use of wearable sensors. These works used the tri-axial accelerometer, ambient/fusion, vibrations or audio and video to capture the human posture, body shape change. However, wearable sensors require relative strict positioning and thus bring along inconvenience especially in the scenario of healthcare unit where elderly seniors may even forget to wear them.

Motivated by the need and importance of image based action detection system we introduce a novel Single Run Action detector (S-RAD) for activity monitoring. S-RAD provides end-to-end action detection without the use of computationally heavy methods in a single shot manner with the ability to run real-time on embedded edge device. S-RAD detects and localizes complex human actions with a Faster-RCNN like architecture [21] combined with temporal shift blocks (based on [14]) to capture the low-level and high-level video temporal context. S-RAD is a privacy-preserving approach and inherently protects Personally Identifiable Information (PII). The real-time execution on edge avoids unnecessary video transfer and PII to a cloud or remote computing server.

Overall, our contributions are as follows: (1) We introduce S-RAD, a single shot action detector localising humans and classifying actions. (2) We demonstrate that we can achieve comparable accuracy to the State-of-the-Art approaches (on the UCF-Sports and UR Fall datasets) at much lower computation cost. We demonstrate our approach on two different dataset from healthcare and sport domain to prove it's robustness and applicability to multiple action detection domains. (3) We additionally provide possibility's of extending our network to real-time scenarios on an edge device. Code is publicly available on GitHub.[1]

---

[1] https://github.com/TeCSAR-UNCC/S-RAD-ActionLocalizationClassification.

2   Related Works

2.1   Activity Recognition Using Wearable Sensors

Most prior research focuses on using wearable and mobile devices (e.g., smartphones, smartwatches) for activity recognition. In designing efficient activity recognition systems, researchers have extensively studied various wearable computing research questions. These research efforts have revolved around optimal placement of the wearable sensors [2], automatic detection of the on-body location of the sensor [22], minimization of the sensing energy consumption [19], and optimization of the power consumption [17]. A limitation of activity monitoring using wearable sensors and mobile devices is that these technologies are battery-powered and therefore need to be regularly charged. Failure to charge the battery results in discontinuity of the activity recognition, which in turn may lead to important behavioral events remaining undetected.

2.2   Action Recognition in Video Data

Action recognition is a long-term research problem and has been studied for decades. Existing State-of-the-Art methods mostly focus on modelling the temporal dependencies in the successive video frames [23,25,26]. For instance, [26] directly averaged the motion cues depicted in different temporal segments in order to capture the irregular nature of temporal information. [23] proposed a two-stream network, which takes RGB frames and optical flows as input respectively and fused the detection's from the two streams as the final output. This was done at several granularities of abstraction and achieved great performance. Beyond multi-stream based methods, methods like [16,25] explored 3D ConvNets on video streams for joint spatio-temporal feature learning on videos. In this way, they avoid calculating the optical flow, keypoints or saliency maps explicitly. However all the above approaches are too large to fit in a real-time edge device. On the other hand [1] uses features calculated from variations in the human keypoints to classify falling and not falling actions, [3] uses VGG16 based on Multi-stream (optical flow, RGB, pose estimation) for human action classification. The above approaches only concentrate on the classification of single human action at scene level and will not perform well if multiple human's are present in an image, which is essential for the healthcare and other public place monitoring systems. Our proposed approach performs human detection and action classification together in a single shot manner where algorithm first localises the human's in an image and classifies his/her action.

2.3   Spatio-Temporal Human Action Detection

Spatio-temporal human action detection is a challenging computer vision problem, which involves detecting human actions in a video as well as localizing these actions both spatially and temporally. Few papers on spatio-temporal action detection like [10] uses object detectors like SSD [15] to generate spatio-temporal tubes by deploying high level linking algorithm on frame level detection's. Inspired by RCNN approaches, [20] used Faster-RCNN [21] to detect the human in an image by capturing the action motion cues with the help of optical flow and classify the final human actions based on the actionness score. [7] extracted proposals by using the selective search method on RGB frames and then applied the original R-CNN on per frame RGB and optical flow data for frame-level action detection's and finally link those detection's using the Viterbi algorithm to generate action tubes. On the other hand [9] uses 3D CNN to generate spatio-temporal tubes with Tube of interest pooling and had showed good performance in the action related datasets. However all these methods poses high processing time and computation cost due to optical flow generation in the two stream networks, 3D kernels in the 3D CNN related works and generation of keypoint's in the human pose based methods. As such, the aforementioned methods are unable to be applied in real-time monitoring systems.

3   Single Run-Action Detector

Approach. We introduce S-RAD, an agile and real-time activity monitoring system. Our approach unifies spatio-temporal feature extraction and localization into a single network, allowing the opportunity to be deployed on edge device. This "on-the-edge" deployment eliminates the need for sending sensitive human data to privacy invalidating cloud servers, similar to [18]. Instead our approach can delete all video data after it is processed and can store only the high level activity analytics. Without stored images, S-RAD can be used to solely focus on differentiating between the human actions rather than identifying or describing the human.

In order to achieve this privacy preserving edge execution, it is important to have an algorithm able to perform in a resource constrained edge environment. Traditionally such constraints resulted in either accuracy reduction, or increased latency. The overview of S-RAD is shown in Fig. 1. S-RAD takes an input sequence of N frames $f_1, f_2, f_3, ..., f_N$ and outputs the detected bounding box and confidence score per each class of the proposals. The model consists of a base feature extractor integrated with temporal shift blocks to capture low level spatio-temporal features. The base feature extractor is made up of the first 40 layers of the original ResNet-50 [8] backbone. The base feature maps are processed by the Region Proposal Network (RPN) using a sliding window approach with handpicked anchors and generates action proposals for each frame. An RPN is a fully convolutional network that simultaneously predicts action bounds and actionness scores at each position. The RPN is trained end-to-end to localize and detect valid region action proposals (the foreground) from background. This sliding window approach to generate the proposals is the source of its accuracy as opposed to SSD's [15] rigid grid base proposal generation.

Following the first stage, the original spatio-temporal base features, in conjecture with the proposals are passed into the Region of interest Align (ROI-Align)

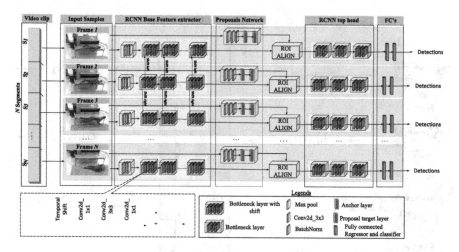

Fig. 1. Overview of the activity detector. Given a sequence of frames we extract channel shifted convolutional features from the base feature extractor to derive the *activity proposals* in the action proposal network. We then ROI align the activity proposals to predict their scores and regress their co-ordinates.

layer which aligns the varying sized action proposals in to a fixed 7×7 spatial sized action proposals. The second stage of the action detector further classifies each valid action proposals to the action classes in that particular frame. The final classification layer outputs $C+1$ scores for each action proposal, one per each action class plus one for the background. The regression layer outputs 4 x K where K is the number of action proposals generated in each frame.

Temporal shift block. TSM [14] are highly hardware efficient. Temporal shift blocks are inserted into the bottleneck layer of Resnet-50 [8] based feature extractor to sustain the spatial information using the identity mapping along with the temporal information using the shifted features. As shown in Fig. 2, each shift receives the C channels from the previous layer. We shift 1/8th of the channels from the past frame to the current frame and shift 1/8th of the channels from current frame to the future frame, while the other part of the channels remain unshifted. The new features (channels are referred to as features) $\hat{x}_2$, have the information of both the past x_1 and future x_2 frames after the "shift" operation. The features are convoluted and mixed into new spatio-temporal features. The shift block coupled to the next layer will do the same operation. Each shift block increases the temporal receptive field by a magnitude of 2 neighbor frames until N frames. For our work we choose $N = 8$ since features are in the magnitude of 8 in Resnet-50 architecture [8].

S-RAD goes beyond action classification to action detection. This is valuable for communal areas such as mesh halls, and for interactions with other human's and with objects. We chose Faster-RCNN [21] as our detection baseline due to its fine-grained detection capabilities when compared to SSD [15]. This fine grained

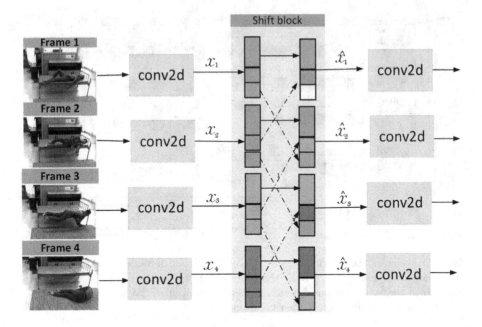

Fig. 2. Temporal shift block

detection is especially applicable to the healthcare domain when dealing with wandering patients and fine-grain abnormal behaviors. Despite the complexity of such tasks our utilization of TSM [14] enables the extraction of the necessary spatio-temporal features for human action localization and individual action classification, in a streaming real-time manner while maintaining privacy.

3.1   Training Loss

RPN Loss: For training RPNs, we assign a binary action class label (of being an action or not i.e foreground vs background) to each anchor. We assign a positive action class label to two kinds of anchors: (i) the anchors with the highest Intersection-over Union (IoU) overlap with a ground-truth box, or (ii) an anchor that has an IoU > 0.7 with any ground-truth box. We assign a negative action class label to a non-positive anchor if it's IoU < 0.3 for all ground-truth boxes. Anchors that are neither positive nor negative do not contribute to the training. With these definitions, our loss function for RPN is defined as:

$$L_{rpn}(\{p_i\}, \{bb_i\}) = \frac{1}{K} \cdot \sum_{i=1}^{K} L_{cls}(p_i, p_i^*) + \frac{1}{K} \cdot \sum_{i=1}^{K} p_i^* L_{reg}(bb_i, bb_i^*) \qquad (1)$$

Here, i is the index of an anchor in a mini-batch and p_i is the predicted probability of anchor i belonging to an action class. The ground-truth label p_i^* is 1 if the anchor is positive, and 0 if the anchor is negative. The vector representing the

4 coordinates of the predicted bounding box is bb_i, and bb_i^* is the ground-truth box associated with a positive anchor. The term p_i^* L_{reg} dictates the smooth L1 regression loss is activated only for positive anchors ($p_i^* = 1$) and is disabled otherwise ($p_i^* = 0$). L_{cls} is log loss(cross-entropy) over two classes (action vs. no action) and is averaged over K frames.

RCNN Loss: The seconds stage of the detector assigns the action class label to the region of interest or foreground proposals from the RPN training. It involves classification loss and regression loss. The classification layer here includes detecting the correct action class label for the proposals from ROI align layer and regression layer is to regress the detected box with ground truth. The RCNN loss is defined as:

$$L_{rcnn}(\{p_i\}, \{bb_i\}) = \tfrac{1}{K} \cdot \sum_{i=1}^{K} L_{cls}(p_i, p_i^*) + \tfrac{1}{K} \cdot \sum_{i=1}^{K} L_{reg}(bb_i, bb_i^*) \qquad (2)$$

where i is the index of proposals or region of interests with spatial dimension 7x7 and p_i is the predicted probability of the action class label, with p_i^* being the ground truth class label. The vector representing the 4 coordinates of the predicted bounding box is bb_i, and bb_i^* is that of the ground-truth box. L_{cls} is log loss (cross-entropy) over multi-classes, L_{reg} is the smooth L1 regression loss and is averaged over K frames. In training mode we set the network to output 256 proposals and in inference mode network outputs 300 proposals.

Total Training Loss: Total loss is defined as sum of RCNN and RPN loss:

$$L_{total} = L_{rpn}(\{p_i\}, \{bb_i\}) + L_{rcnn}(\{p_i\}, \{bb_i\}) \qquad (3)$$

4   Results and Evaluations

Setup. We use Resnet-50 [8] as the backbone of our architecture because of the network depth and residual connections that enable feature reuse and propagation. The UCF-Sports [24] and UR Fall [12] datasets are too small and are prone to over fitting, so we fine-tuned our network from Kinetics [11] pre-trained weights and froze the batch normalization layers. The training parameters for the UCF-Sports [24] dataset are 300 training epochs, with an inital learning rate of 0.03 and a weight decay 0.1 every 60 epochs. We utilized gradient accumulation with a batch size of 4 and an accumulation step of 3 to fit a total batch of 12 on one V100GPU. The training parameters for the UR Fall dataset [12] are 80 training epochs, with initial learning rate of 0.02 and a weight decay 0.1 every 20 epochs. We use the uniform temporal sampling strategy done in [26] to sample 8 frames from the video and resize the input resolution of the image to 300×400 for State-of-the-Art comparison. We used datasets from two different domain (Sport and Healthcare) to show the generic capability of our algorithm.

4.1   Results on UCF-Sports Dataset

The UCF-Sports dataset [24] consists of 150 videos from 10 action classes. All videos have spatio-temporal annotations in the form of frame-level bounding boxes and we follow the same training/testing split used by [7]. On average there are 103 videos in the training dataset and 47 videos in the testing dataset. Videos are truncated to the action and bounding boxes annotations are provided for all frames. To quantify our results, we report the mean Average Precision (mAP) at the frame level (frame mAP). Frame-level metrics allow us to compare the quality of the detection's independently. We use the Precision-recall AUC (Area under curve) to calculate the average precision per class. We compute the mean of the average precision per class to see how much our algorithm is able to differentiate the features between action classes. We followed the same procedure as in the PASCAL VOC detection challenge [6] to have an apple to apple comparison with the State-of-the-Art approaches in the detection task. We first evaluate S-RAD on the widely used UCF-Sports dataset. Table 1 indicates frame level Average Precision per class for an intersection-over-union threshold of 0.5. Our approach achieves a mean AP of 85.04%. While obtaining excellent performance on most of the classes, walking is the only action for which the framework fails to detect the humans (40.71% frame-AP). This is possibly due to several factors, the first being that the test videos for "walking" contain multiple actors in close proximity, which results in false detections due to occlusions. Additionally, walking is a very slow action with fine grained features and potentially lacks enough temporal displacement in 8 frames to be picked up by our detector due to sparse temporal sampling strategy. Ultimately, our approach is off by only 2% when compared to the State-of-the-Art approaches that utilize either multi-modal, 3-dimensional, or complex proposal architecture solutions. The State-of-the-Art comparison in terms of mean Average precision (mAP) is summarised in Table 2.

Table 1. State-of-the-Art per class frame mAP comparison in UCF-Sports

Action class	[7]	[27]	[20]	[9]	S-RAD
Diving	75.79	60.71	96.12	84.37	**99.90**
Golf	69.29	77.54	80.46	90.79	87.20
Kicking	54.60	65.26	73.48	86.48	76.00
Lifting	99.09	100.00	99.17	99.76	**99.96**
Riding	89.59	99.53	97.56	100.0	**99.90**
Run	54.89	52.60	82.37	83.65	**89.79**
Skate Boarding	29.80	47.14	57.43	68.71	67.93
Swing1	88.70	88.87	83.64	65.75	**88.78**
Swing2	74.50	62.85	98.50	99.71	**99.9**
Walk	44.70	64.43	75.98	87.79	40.71

Table 2. Overall frame mAP at IOU 0.5 threshold comparison in UCF-Sports Action dataset

	[7]	[27]	[20]	[9]	[10]	[5]	S-RAD
mAP	68.09	71.90	84.51	86.70	**87.7**	83.9	85.04

The Precision Recall AUC is ploted in Fig. 3 shows the capability of our algorithm to separate different classes.

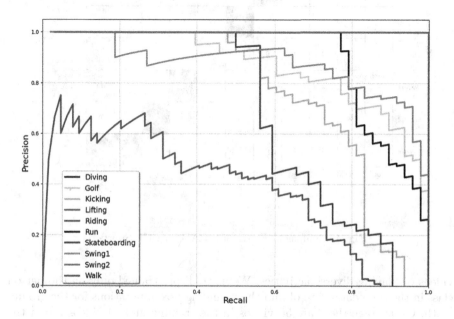

Fig. 3. Precision-Recall curve per Action class in UCF-Sports

We also provided the confusion matrix to better understand the detections with the original ground truth in Fig. 4. The confusion matrix is calculated considering both the detection and classification tasks. Here the grids in the diagonal are the true positive's whose IOU > 0.5 and the detected action class label match with the ground truth action class label. Other columns are the false positive whose IOU > 0.5 but the detected action class label does not match the ground truth action class label. The last column contains false negatives with detections with an IOU < 0.5.

4.2   Results on UR Fall Dataset

We have also evaluated our framework on the healthcare extensive dataset [12]. The UR Fall dataset is composed of 70 videos: (i) 30 videos of falls; and (ii) 40

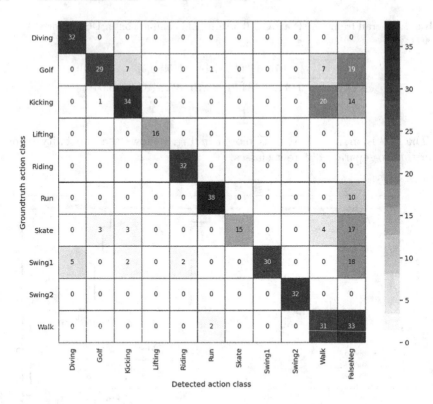

Fig. 4. Confusion matrix of S-RAD on UCF-Sports

videos displaying diverse activities. We used [4] pre-trained only on the person class in the coco dataset to obtain the bounding box annotations for the ground truth. On average there are 56 videos in the training and 14 videos are in the testing dataset.

For the UR Fall dataset we calculate specificity, sensitivity and accuracy along with mAP for comparison.

(1) Sensitivity: A metric to evaluate detecting falls. And compute the ratio of trues positives to the number of falls.

$$Sensitivity = \frac{TP}{TP + FN} * 100 \qquad (4)$$

(2) Specificity: A metric to evaluate how much our algorithm detects just "fall" and avoids misclassification with the "not fall" class.

$$Specificity = \frac{TN}{TN + FP} * 100 \qquad (5)$$

(3) Accuracy: Metric to compute how much our algorithm can differ between falls and non-fall videos.

$$Accuracy = \frac{TP + TN}{TN + FP + TP + FN} * 100 \qquad (6)$$

True positive (TP) means that the frame has a fall and our algorithm has detected fall in those frames. True negative (TN) refers to the frames that don't contain fall and our algorithm does not detect fall in those frames. False negative (FN) designates the frames containing falls, however our algorithm fails to detect the fall in those frames. Finally, false positive (FP) indicates the frames don't contain a fall, yet our algorithm claims to detect a fall. For the sake of comparison with the other classification based State-of-the-Art papers we take the detection with the highest confidence score from the output of S-RAD and compare it's class label with the ground truth class label to calculate the above mentioned parameters. Since our approach is based on frame level detection, the classification task on UR fall dataset is also done in frame level. We achieved a competitive score of 96.54 % in mAP (detection task at frame level). It is important to note, other State-of-the-Art approaches on this dataset relied solely on classification, hence our comparison being concentrated on the classification metrics. The Results are shown on Table 3, showing S-RAD's true capabilities in the field of healthcare.

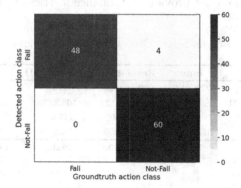

Fig. 5. Confusion matrix of S-RAD on UR Fall dataset

The confusion matrix on Fig. 5 shows the ability of the S-RAD to distinguish Fall and Not Fall with only 4 instances being misclassified as Fall.

Table 3. State-of-the-Art per frame comparison in UR Fall dataset

	[1]	[16]	[3]	[13]	**S-RAD**
Sensitivity	100	-	100	100	**100**
Specificity	95	-	98.61	98.77	**93.75**
Accuracy	97.5	99.27	98.77	98.84	**96.46**

4.3 Real-Time Execution

The S-RAD framework has the advantage of reduced inference time and less number of parameters, enabling us to perform real-time on the edge activity monitoring in a privacy-aware manner. We compare our framework with others in terms of FPS (Frame-Per-Second) and mAP in Table 4 on the UCF-Sports Action dataset. We tested our models on one Titan V GPU (except the work of TubeCNN [9], which was reported on a titan X). The trade-off is between accuracy and inference FPS, as well as parameters. Among the state of the art approaches, our method has the second fastest run time and can process 41 frames per second which is three times faster than [9] and [20]. Moreover, the number of parameters of our framework is the smallest, about 28.36 M in Table 4, although works like [5] have better FPS with their models, their features are too heavy to fit into a real-time edge device, additionally our work maintains a higher mAP at a high resolution when compared to their work. We were unable to provide performance comparisons with the State-of-the-Art approaches on the UR Fall dataset as most of the approaches are not publicly available to run on the edge device, and do not provide performance metrics of their own.

Table 4. Comparison on Server Class Execution on Nvidia Titan platform

Approach	Input	Resolution	Param # (M)	FPS	mAP
Multi-stream [20]	RGB+Flow	600 × 1067	274	11.82	84.51
CapsuleNet[5]	RGB	112 × 112	103.137	78.41	83.9
TubeCNN[9]	RGB	300 × 400	245.87	17.391	86.7
ACT[10]	RGB+Flow	300 × 300	50	12	87.7
S-RAD	**RGB**	**300 × 400**	**28.35**	**41.64**	**85.04**

We additionally evaluated our work on an edge platform, the Nvidia Xavier to test its performance on an resource constrained edge platform. We compare the work of VideoCapsuleNet [5] with our approach, and despite their initial performance advantage on the Titan V, our work is the only model capable of running on the memory constrained edge device. S-RAD, as opposed to Video-CapsuleNet folds temporal data into the channel dimension, and as a result avoids introducing another dimension to the tensor sizes. VideoCapsuleNet not only process 3D spatial-temporal feature maps, but they also introduce another dimension of complexity in the form of capsules. We also observed 6.0 FPS with 5.21 W of total SoC (on chip) power consumption.

5 Conclusion

This paper introduced a novel Single Run Action detector (S-RAD) for activity monitoring. S-RAD provides end-to-end action detection without the use of computationally heavy methods with the ability for real-time execution of embedded edge devices. S-RAD is a privacy-preserving approach and inherently protects Personally Identifiable Information (PII). Results on UCF-Sports and UR Fall dataset presented comparable accuracy to State-of-the-Art approaches with significantly lower model size and computation demand and the ability for real-time execution on edge embedded device.

References

1. Alaoui, A.Y., El Fkihi, S., Thami, R.O.H.: Fall detection for elderly people using the variation of key points of human skeleton. IEEE Access **7**, 154786–154795 (2019)
2. Atallah, L., Lo, B., King, R., Yang, G.Z.: Sensor positioning for activity recognition using wearable accelerometers. IEEE Trans. Biomed. Circ. Syst. **5**(4), 320–329 (2011)
3. Cameiro, S.A., da Silva, G.P., Leite, G.V., Moreno, R., Guimarães, S.J.F., Pedrini, H.: Multi-stream deep convolutional network using high-level features applied to fall detection in video sequences. In: 2019 International Conference on Systems, Signals and Image Processing (IWSSIP), pp. 293–298 (2019)
4. Chen, K., et al.: MMDetection: Open mmlab detection toolbox and benchmark. arXiv preprint arXiv:1906.07155 (2019)
5. Duarte, K., Rawat, Y.S., Shah, M.: Videocapsulenet: a simplified network for action detection. In: Proceedings of the 32nd International Conference on Neural Information Processing Systems, NIPS 2018, pp. 7621–7630. Curran Associates Inc., Red Hook (2018)
6. Everingham, M., Gool, L., Williams, C.K., Winn, J., Zisserman, A.: The pascal visual object classes (voc) challenge. Int. J. Comput. Vision **88**(2), 303–338 (2010). https://doi.org/10.1007/s11263-009-0275-40275-4
7. Gkioxari et al., Georgia, J.M.: Finding action tubes. CoRR abs/1411.6031 (2014). http://arxiv.org/abs/1411.6031
8. He, K., Zhang, X., Ren, S., Sun, J.: Deep residual learning for image recognition. CoRR abs/1512.03385 (2015). http://arxiv.org/abs/1512.03385
9. Hou, R., Chen, C., Shah, M.: Tube convolutional neural network (t-cnn) for action detection in videos. In: The IEEE International Conference on Computer Vision (ICCV), October 2017
10. Kalogeiton, V., Weinzaepfel, P., Ferrari, V., Schmid, C.: Action tubelet detector for spatio-temporal action localization. CoRR abs/1705.01861 (2017). http://arxiv.org/abs/1705.01861
11. Kay, W., et al.: The kinetics human action video dataset. arXiv preprint arXiv:1705.06950 (2017)
12. Kwolek, B., Kepski, M.: Human fall detection on embedded platform using depth maps and wireless accelerometer. Comput. Methods Programs Biomed. **117**(3), 489–501 (2014)
13. Leite, G., Silva, G., Pedrini, H.: Fall detection in video sequences based on a three-stream convolutional neural network. In: 2019 18th IEEE International Conference On Machine Learning and Applications (ICMLA), pp. 191–195 (2019)
14. Lin, J., Gan, C., Han, S.: Temporal shift module for efficient video understanding. CoRR abs/1811.08383 (2018). http://arxiv.org/abs/1811.08383
15. Liu, W., et al.: SSD: single shot multibox detector. CoRR abs/1512.02325 (2015). http://arxiv.org/abs/1512.02325

16. Lu, N., Wu, Y., Feng, L., Song, J.: Deep learning for fall detection: three-dimensional CNN combined with LSTM on video kinematic data. IEEE J. Biomed. Health Inform. **23**(1), 314–323 (2019)
17. Mirzadeh, S.I., Ghasemzadeh, H.: Optimal policy for deployment of machine learning models on energy-bounded systems. In: Proceedings of the Twenty-Ninth International Joint Conference on Artificial Intelligence (IJCAI) (2020)
18. Neff, C., Mendieta, M., Mohan, S., Baharani, M., Rogers, S., Tabkhi, H.: Revamp2t: real-time edge video analytics for multicamera privacy-aware pedestrian tracking. IEEE Internet Things J. **7**(4), 2591–2602 (2020)
19. Pagan, J., et al.: Toward ultra-low-power remote health monitoring: an optimal and adaptive compressed sensing framework for activity recognition. IEEE Trans. Mobile Comput. (TMC) **18**(3), 658–673 (2018)
20. Peng et al., Xiaojiang, S.C.: Multi-region two-stream R-CNN for action detection. Lecture Notes in Computer Science, vol. 9908, pp. 744–759. Springer, Amsterdam, Netherlands, October 2016. https://doi.org/10.1007/978-3-319-46493-0_45, https://hal.inria.fr/hal-01349107
21. Ren, S., He, K., Girshick, R.B., Sun, J.: Faster R-CNN: towards real-time object detection with region proposal networks. CoRR abs/1506.01497 (2015). http://arxiv.org/abs/1506.01497
22. Saeedi, R., Purath, J., Venkatasubramanian, K., Ghasemzadeh, H.: Toward seamless wearable sensing: automatic on-body sensor localization for physical activity monitoring. In: 2014 36th Annual International Conference of the IEEE Engineering in Medicine and Biology Society, pp. 5385–5388. IEEE (2014)
23. Simonyan, K., Zisserman, A.: Two-stream convolutional networks for action recognition in videos. CoRR abs/1406.2199 (2014). http://arxiv.org/abs/1406.2199
24. Soomro, K., Zamir, A.R.: Action recognition in realistic sports videos (2014)
25. Tran, D., Bourdev, L.D., Fergus, R., Torresani, L., Paluri, M.: C3D: generic features for video analysis. CoRR abs/1412.0767 (2014). http://arxiv.org/abs/1412.0767
26. Wang, L., Xiong, Y., Wang, Z., Qiao, Y., Lin, D., Tang, X., Gool, L.V.: Temporal segment networks: Towards good practices for deep action recognition. CoRR abs/1608.00859 (2016). http://arxiv.org/abs/1608.00859
27. Weinzaepfel, P., Harchaoui, Z., Schmid, C.: Learning to track for spatio-temporal action localization. CoRR abs/1506.01929 (2015). http://arxiv.org/abs/1506.01929

Efficacy of Model Fine-Tuning for Personalized Dynamic Gesture Recognition

Junyao Guo$^{(\boxtimes)}$ (ID), Unmesh Kurup (ID), and Mohak Shah (ID)

Advanced AI, America Research Lab, LG Electronics, Santa Clara, USA
{junyao.guo,unmesh.kurup,mohak.shah}@lge.com

Abstract. Dynamic hand gestures are usually unique to individual users in terms of style, speed, and magnitude of the gestures' performance. A gesture recognition model trained with data from a group of users may not generalize well for unseen users and its performance is likely to be different for different users. To address these issues, this paper investigates the approach of fine-tuning a global model using user-specific data locally for personalizing dynamic hand gesture recognition. Using comprehensive experiments with state-of-the-art convolutional neural network architectures for video recognition, we evaluate the impact of four different choices on personalization performance - fine-tuning the earlier vs the later layers of the network, number of user-specific training samples, batch size, and learning rate. The user-specific data is collected from 11 users performing 7 gesture classes. Our findings show that with proper selection of fine-tuning strategy and hyperparameters, improved model performance can be achieved on personalized models for all users by only fine-tuning a small portion of the network weights and using very few labeled user-specific training samples.

Keywords: Model personalization · Dynamic gesture recognition · Model fine-tuning · Light-weight convolutional neural network · Hyperparameter tuning

1 Introduction

Dynamic hand gesture recognition provides a natural user interface for various applications including autonomous driving, smart homes, and robotics. The state-of-the-art approaches for gesture recognition use deep neural networks (DNNs) trained on large-scale datasets, which are usually collected via RGB or depth cameras. These models are then deployed directly on users' devices for inference without further changes. However, significant variances exist among users in terms of style, speed, hand used (left vs right), and magnitude when performing a gesture [1,17]. As a consequence, a single generic model trained on global data may not always generalize well and could exhibit very different performances for each individual user.

© Springer Nature Singapore Pte Ltd. 2021
X. Li et al. (Eds.): DL-HAR 2020, CCIS 1370, pp. 99–110, 2021.
https://doi.org/10.1007/978-981-16-0575-8_8

To enhance model performance (while also preserving the user's privacy), a model personalization approach is needed that adapts the model to user-specific data locally. A common approach for DNN model personalization is to fine-tune a pre-trained global model using only local user data. This approach has been used for personalizing keyboard input prediction [16] and speech recognition [14]. However, it has not been reported whether fine-tuning is effective for personalized video recognition tasks such as dynamic gesture recognition.

Therefore, in this paper, we assess the efficacy of fine-tuning for dynamic gesture recognition personalization. To the best of our knowledge, this is the first systematic empirical study on exploring a fine-tuning approach for DNN model personalization on video data. Specifically, our contributions are 1) collecting a proprietary gesture dataset from 11 users, 2) conducting comprehensive experiments on four state-of-the-art light-weight convolutional neural network (CNN) architectures, and 3) studying the impact of multiple hyperparameters on fine-tuning, including number of fine-tuned parameters, early or late layers to fine-tune, number of user-specific training samples, batch size, and learning rate.

Our findings show that by choosing these hyperparameters properly, recognition accuracy gain can be achieved for all users after fine-tuning by using very few labelled user data and updating a small number of network parameters. Particularly, we make the following three key observations: 1) fine-tuning early layers can achieve similar accuracy gain as fine-tuning late layers but with significantly fewer parameters to be fine-tuned; 2) as few as one or two user specific training samples per gesture class can improve the recognition accuracy with fine-tuning; and 3) fine-tuning shows good convergence with small batch sizes such as 2 or 4. These findings indicate that fine-tuning is a promising approach for training personalized video recognition models on-device to enhance user experience.

2   Related Works

Personalization has mostly been studied under the federated learning (FL) framework, where the global model is trained via federated averaging [12]. In [15], a recurrent neural network model is personalized by fine-tuning the global model on user data locally, where impacts of training batch-size and learning rate are evaluated. Another work [5] combined federated averaging with a meta learning algorithm to improve the model performance after personalization. [13] proposed an approach for personalizing a global model while still preserving its performance on general data. The way to achieve this improvement is to combine on-device training with random rehearsal and server-side model averaging. [9] presented the first learning-theoretic study of personalization under the FL framework and proposed user clustering, data interpolation, and model interpolation as three efficient algorithms for personalization. However, in this paper, we will not follow the FL approach, as video recognition models generally need massive data to train and the performance of FL has not been well evaluated given that video data is scarce on each user's device. Also, we assume that the user model after personalization will stay on-device and will not be used for updating the global model.

A recent work [11] applies an adaptive batch normalization for domain adaptation method in personalized human activity recognition. This method adapts a CNN model to unseen target users by updating the user-specific batch normalization layers. However, the proposed approach requires that during the training of the initial model, each batch should only contain training samples from one user, which is not required by the fine-tuning approach studied in this paper.

In the application field, DNN model personalization is studied for keyboard input prediction [16], handwritten character recognition [3], speech recognition [14], and gaze estimation [4]. Compared to these applications, gesture recognition, particularly, dynamic gesture recognition using camera data requires video sequence analysis, which generally needs more complex models that are harder to fine-tune on-device. Consequently, studies on gesture recognition personalization either use traditional machine learning approaches [1,2] whose performances are inferior to DNN-based approaches or use skeleton data [6,17] which are not easy to obtain and label by users.

However, with recent advances in light-weight DNN architectures for video recognition, gesture recognition can be run in real-time on embedded GPUs and mobile devices [7,8]. This brings the opportunity of personalizing video recognition on-device and motivates this work on evaluation of personalization strategies on video sequences.

3   Method

3.1   User Dataset

Seven classes are considered in this work, namely, swiping left, swiping right, pulling hand in, pushing hand away, thumb up, zooming out with full hand and no gesture. These gestures are a subset of the 27 classes from the Jester dataset [10]. We used a laptop RGB camera to record video clips of 11 users, who were asked to perform these gestures without expert demonstration. The videos were recorded under the same environmental setting and lighting for all users. For each gesture class, 6 to 10 samples were collected from each user, and every user has the same number of samples per class. In total, 52 samples per user will be used for these experiments. Note that currently there is no similar dataset available for benchmark which groups the dynamic hand gesture videos by users. Therefore, we only conduct experiments on our collected user dataset.

3.2   Global Model Training

We evaluate 4 state-of-the-art CNNs that can run fast video recognition on embedded GPUs, namely, 3D-MobileNetV2-1.0x, 3D-SqueezeNet, 3D-ShuffleNetV2-0.25x [7], and MobileNetV2-1.0x with temporal shift module [8] (denoted as MobileNetV2-TSM). The global models are first trained with the selected group of gestures from the Jester dataset, which will be referred to as general data. To ensure a good baseline performance for these global models, we did hyperparameter tuning for training and present the best hyperparameters as follows. The training stops after 50 epochs. The initial learning rate is set to 0.01 for SqueezeNet whereas 0.1 for the other models, with a decay factor of 0.1 at epoch 20 and 40. Stochastic gradient descent is used with weight decay 0.0001 for MobileNetV2-TSM and 0.001 for other models. Batch size is 16 and dropout is 0.5 for the fully connected layer. The global models' sizes, speeds and accuracies are listed in Table 1. Note that all global models have an accuracy drop on user data, which could be partially caused by the differences in environmental settings in the global training data.

Table 1. Global model performances. *Params* is the total trainable parameters of the model for 7 gesture classes. *Speed* measures the time on running one forward-pass for one video clip of 16 frames and size 112×112 on the Nvidia TITAN Xp GPU averaged over 3000 runs. *Acc* measures the accuracy on the global Jester validation set and *Acc User* measures the average prediction accuracy on all samples collected from all users.

Model	Params	Speed	Acc	Acc user
MobileNetV2-TSM	2.23M	10 ms	0.975	0.925
3D-MobileNetV2	2.36M	99 ms	0.970	0.864
3D-SqueezeNet	1.84M	6 ms	0.953	0.836
3D-ShuffleNetV2	0.22M	30 ms	0.933	0.809

3.3   Data Augmentation

For both global model training and fine-tuning, the following data augmentation methods are used. For temporal augmentation, for training, 16 frames are randomly selected from a video sample while maintaining their original order, whereas for validation, 16 consecutive frames are selected from the center of the video. For spatial augmentation, for training, each frame is randomly cropped with size 112×112 and rescaled randomly with one of the factors in $[1, 0.875, 0.766, 0.67]$, whereas for validation, a center crop resized to 112×112 is used. In each epoch, only one clip from each video input is sampled and used.

3.4   Personalization Strategy

For each user, a personalized model is obtained by fine-tuning partial or all of the network weights initialized from the global model. A personalization strategy consists of the hyperparameters for fine-tuning, including parameters/layers to fine-tune, number of training samples, batch size and learning rate. A personalized model is obtained by fine-tuning the global model for 20 epochs given the personalization strategy.

We experiment with different numbers of fined-tuned layers according to the model architecture. The models usually consist of some type of blocks (e.g., convolution block, inverted residual block for MobileNetV2, Fire block for SqueezeNet, etc). For the same type of block that is repeated multiple times consecutively, we either fine-tune all or none of them. We consider two fine-tuning strategies - fine-tuning early layers and fine-tuning late layers. More specifically, fine-tuning early layers means that we fine-tune a certain number of layers from the beginning of the network while keeping the weights of the later layers frozen and vice versa when fine-tuning the late layers.

3.5   Metric

To evaluate the benefit of model personalization, delta accuracy is used to measure the performance of a personalization strategy. Similar to [15], the delta accuracy is calculated by the following steps for each user: 1) The user data is split randomly into training and test sets, where the training set includes K samples per class and the test set includes the rest of the samples; 2) The global model is applied to the test set and the accuracy is noted as *accuracy-before-finetune*; 3) The global model is finetuned using the user training set and accuracy is recorded on the test set as *accuracy-after-finetune*; 4) The delta accuracy is calculated as *accuracy-after-finetune − accuracy-before-finetune*. We summarize these metric measurement steps in Fig. 1.

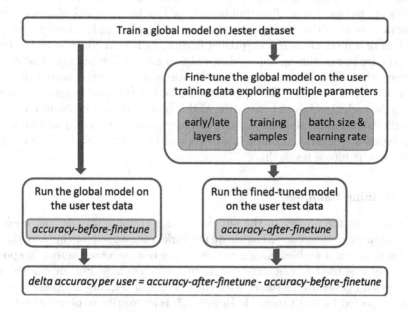

Fig. 1. Experiment flowchart and metric measurement.

For each user, we conduct the steps illustrated in Fig. 1 for 5 trials and report the average of delta accuracies of all trials. To measure the overall performance of a personalization strategy, the mean of delta accuracies across all users is used.

4 Experiments

4.1 Fine-Tuned Layers

The first experiment shows the impact of fine-tuning strategies, specifically, fine-tuning early or late layers and number of fine-tuned layers, on the personalization performance. The results are shown in Fig. 2. The batch size is set to 4, learning rate to 0.001, and the number of training samples per class is 3. The number of fine-tuned layers is represented by the percentage of fine-tuned parameters.

As can be seen in Fig. 2, regardless of whether the early or late layers are fine-tuned, the mean delta accuracy generally increases with the number of fine-tuned layers and the number of training epochs. This result in unsurprising given the increase in learning capacity when more weights are available to be fine-tuned.

Another, more interesting, observation is that for all model architectures, fine-tuning early layers is much more efficient than fine-tuning late layers for similar accuracy gain. This result shows that by capturing the uniqueness of users in low-level features rather than high-level features, the model adapts to individual users more efficiently. We also noticed that the majority of corrected samples are the same after fine-tuning early or late layers, which shows no clear distinction between the user-specific features that early and late layers adapt to. This lack of a distinction is a surprising finding, as it is in contrast to the common practice in fine-tuning approaches which generally fine tune the last couple of layers while assuming the lower-level features are universal across different subjects or even domains. The question of whether this phenomenon is model or data dependent is beyond the scope of this paper and is a problem for future research. Additionally, the runtime and memory consumption for fine-tuning different layers are dependent on the framework and hardware used, which are also subject to our future research.

4.2 Training Samples

Figure 3 shows the impact of the number of user training samples per class on personalization performance. The entire network is fine-tuned for this experiment with batch size of 4 and learning rate 0.001. The best accuracy across 20 epochs for each user is used to calculate the mean delta accuracy. For all models, the accuracy gain generally increases with the number of training samples, which is usually expected for fine-tuning [3]. However, it is interesting to observe that even with only one training sample per class, users can already start to experience notable accuracy gain. This accuracy gain shows that fine-tuning is fairly sample efficient which, in turn, suggests that little user effort is needed for labeling data.

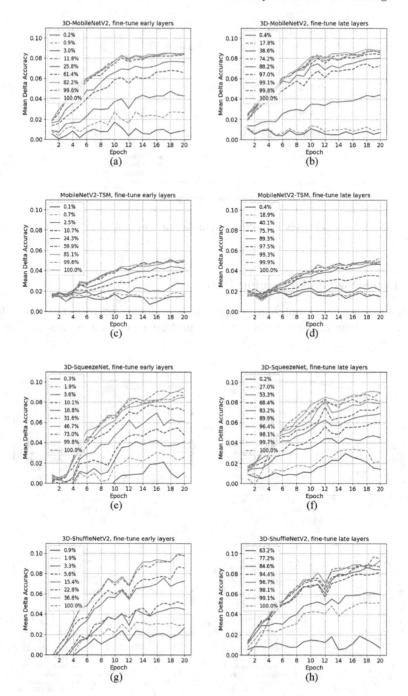

Fig. 2. Mean delta accuracy for different fine-tuning strategies and percentages of fine-tuned parameters. (a)(c)(e)(g): fine-tuning early layers; (b)(d)(f)(h): fine-tuning late layers. The legend denotes the percentage of the total network parameters that are fine-tuned.

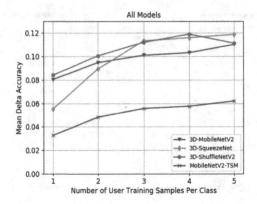

Fig. 3. Mean delta accuracy for different number of user training samples per gesture class.

4.3   Batch Size and Learning Rate

We experimented with batch sizes 1, 2, and 4, and learning rates 0.01 and 0.001 to evaluate their impacts on fine-tuning performance. The results are shown

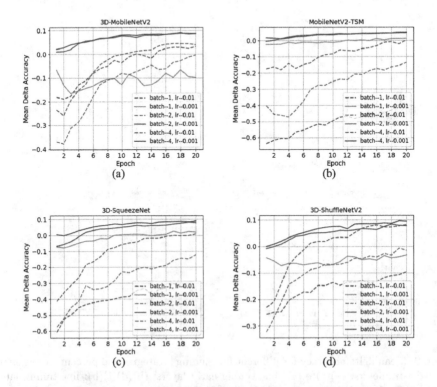

Fig. 4. Mean delta accuracy using different batch sizes and learning rates.

in Fig. 4, with the entire network fine-tuned. As the batch sizes are relatively small, the smaller learning rate 0.001 yields better convergence curve than 0.01. In terms of batch size, the larger the batch size, the better the convergence, which is generally expected in DNN training. Particularly, for 3D-MobileNetV2 and 3D-ShuffleNetV2, using a batch size of 1 will deteriorate the global model performance due to unstable convergence. However, with learning rate 0.001, using a batch size of 2 is only slightly inferior than batch size of 4, while saving on memory for training which could be critical if fine-tuning is implemented on resource constrained devices. We have also experimented with fine-tuning partial network with different batch sizes and learning rates, and obtained the same observation that using the batch size of 2 and 4 with learning rate 0.001 can yield stable convergence for all models.

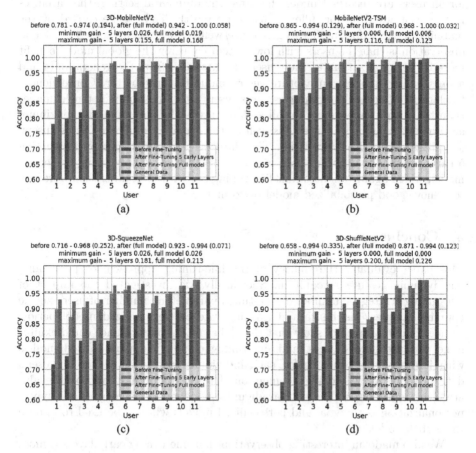

Fig. 5. Accuracy of each user before and after fine-tuning. Accuracy ranges and largest difference among users are shown in the figure titles. (Color figure online)

4.4   Per-User Performance

Figure 5 shows the performance gain for each user by fine-tuning. The users are sorted by accuracy before fine-tuning for better presentation, and the best accuracy over 20 fine-tuning epochs is chosen to be the accuracy after fine-tuning. We show the plot of fine-tuning both the 5 early layers and the entire model using 3 training samples, but the same trends can be observed with other numbers of fine-tuned layers and training samples. The red bar shows the accuracy of global model on the general validation set.

The first observation is that by directly applying the global model to user data, almost all users experience an accuracy drop due to the variance between the user data and the general data indicating the necessity of personalization to improve the global model performance for individual users. As the videos for all users are recorded under the same environmental setting, the variances in the accuracy drop for different users are mostly likely to be caused by the inability of the global model to generalize well to all unseen users. The second observation is that the users with lower accuracy using the global model benefit more by personalization, as these users deviate more from the general data and a personalized model can capture their unique features better. Consequently, the largest difference in accuracies across users after fine-tuning is much smaller than that before fine-tuning for all architectures. The minimum and maximum accuracy gain among all users, as well as the accuracy difference across users, are presented in the figure titles. The third observation is that by fine-tuning 5 early layers, the accuracy gain is very close to that of fine-tuning the entire model, which again validates that fine-tuning early layers is an efficient strategy to achieve good personalized model performance.

5   Conclusion

This paper evaluates the efficacy of the fine-tuning approach for personalizing dynamic gesture recognition. Specifically, we investigated the impact of fine-tuning strategies, number of fine-tuned parameters, number of user-specific training samples, batch-size and learning rate on personalized model performance. Empirical results show that the global model performance could exhibit large variance across users, and fine-tuning could yield personalized models with improved performance for each individual user while preserving user's data privacy. We would like to mention that the fine-tuning approach evaluated here represents a different paradigm from federated learning, where hyper-personalization is the goal and personalized models will not be used to update the global model.

We also made an interesting observation that fine-tuning early layers is more efficient than fine-tuning late layers, which invites further research on how to conduct efficient fine-tuning for various model architectures and datasets. Moreover, we showed that using small batch sizes and few user-specific training samples can achieve good convergence. These findings suggest that fine-tuning could be a viable approach for on-device model personalization for video recognition applications.

References

1. Costante, G., Bellocchio, E., Valigi, P., Ricci, E.: Personalizing vision-based gestural interfaces for HRI with uavs: a transfer learning approach. In: 2014 IEEE/RSJ International Conference on Intelligent Robots and Systems, pp. 3319–3326. IEEE (2014)
2. Costante, G., Galieni, V., Yan, Y., Fravolini, M.L., Ricci, E., Valigi, P.: Exploiting transfer learning for personalized view invariant gesture recognition. In: 2014 IEEE International Conference on Acoustics, Speech and Signal Processing (ICASSP), pp. 1250–1254. IEEE (2014)
3. Harris, B., Bae, I., Egger, B.: Architectures and algorithms for on-device user customization of CNNs. Integration **67**, 121–133 (2019)
4. He, J., et al.: On-device few-shot personalization for real-time gaze estimation. In: Proceedings of the IEEE International Conference on Computer Vision Workshops (2019)
5. Jiang, Y., Konečný, J., Rush, K., Kannan, S.: Improving federated learning personalization via model agnostic meta learning. arXiv preprint arXiv:1909.12488 (2019)
6. Joshi, A., Ghosh, S., Betke, M., Sclaroff, S., Pfister, H.: Personalizing gesture recognition using hierarchical Bayesian neural networks. In: Proceedings of the IEEE Conference on Computer Vision and Pattern Recognition, pp. 6513–6522 (2017)
7. Köpüklü, O., Kose, N., Gunduz, A., Rigoll, G.: Resource efficient 3D convolutional neural networks. arXiv preprint arXiv:1904.02422 (2019)
8. Lin, J., Gan, C., Han, S.: TSM: temporal shift module for efficient video understanding. In: Proceedings of the IEEE International Conference on Computer Vision, pp. 7083–7093 (2019)
9. Mansour, Y., Mohri, M., Ro, J., Suresh, A.T.: Three approaches for personalization with applications to federated learning. arXiv preprint arXiv:2002.10619 (2020)
10. Materzynska, J., Berger, G., Bax, I., Memisevic, R.: The jester dataset: a large-scale video dataset of human gestures. In: Proceedings of the IEEE International Conference on Computer Vision Workshops (2019)
11. Mazankiewicz, A., Böhm, K., Bergés, M.: Incremental real-time personalization in human activity recognition using domain adaptive batch normalization. arXiv preprint arXiv:2005.12178 (2020)
12. McMahan, B., Moore, E., Ramage, D., Hampson, S., y Arcas, B.A.: Communication-efficient learning of deep networks from decentralized data. In: Artificial Intelligence and Statistics, pp. 1273–1282 (2017)
13. Popov, V., Kudinov, M., Piontkovskaya, I., Vytovtov, P., Nevidomsky, A.: Distributed fine-tuning of language models on private data. In: ICLR (2018)
14. Sim, K.C., et al.: Personalization of end-to-end speech recognition on mobile devices for named entities. arXiv preprint arXiv:1912.09251 (2019)
15. Wang, K., Mathews, R., Kiddon, C., Eichner, H., Beaufays, F., Ramage, D.: Federated evaluation of on-device personalization. arXiv preprint arXiv:1910.10252 (2019)

16. Xu, M., Qian, F., Mei, Q., Huang, K., Liu, X.: Deeptype: on-device deep learn-
    ing for input personalization service with minimal privacy concern. Proc. ACM
    Interact. Mob. Wearable Ubiquitous Technol. **2**(4), 1–26 (2018)
17. Yao, A., Van Gool, L., Kohli, P.: Gesture recognition portfolios for personaliza-
    tion. In: Proceedings of the IEEE Conference on Computer Vision and Pattern
    Recognition, pp. 1915–1922 (2014)

Fully Convolutional Network Bootstrapped by Word Encoding and Embedding for Activity Recognition in Smart Homes

Damien Bouchabou[1,2(✉)], Sao Mai Nguyen[1(✉)] [iD], Christophe Lohr[1(✉)], Benoit LeDuc[2(✉)], and Ioannis Kanellos[1(✉)]

[1] IMT Atlantique, Lab-STICC, UMR 6285, 29238 Brest, France
{damien.bouchabou,christophe.lohr,ioannis.kanellos}@imt-atlantique.fr,
nguyensmai@gmail.com
[2] Delta Dore Company, Bonnemain, France
{dbouchabou,bleduc}@deltadore.com

Abstract. Activity recognition in smart homes is essential when we wish to propose automatic services for the inhabitants. However, it is a challenging problem in terms of environments' variability, sensory-motor systems, user habits, but also sparsity of signals and redundancy of models. Therefore, end-to-end systems fail at automatically extracting key features, and need to access context and domain knowledge. We propose to tackle feature extraction for activity recognition in smart homes by merging methods of Natural Language Processing (NLP) and Time Series Classification (TSC) domains.

We evaluate the performance of our method with two datasets issued from the Center for Advanced Studies in Adaptive Systems (CASAS). We analyze the contributions of the use of embedding based on term frequency encoding, to improve automatic feature extraction. Moreover we compare the classification performance of Fully Convolutional Network (FCN) from TSC, applied for the first time for activity recognition in smart homes, to Long Short Term Memory (LSTM). The method we propose, shows good performance in offline activity classification. Our analysis also shows that FCNs outperforms LSTMs, and that domain knowledge gained by event encoding and embedding improves significantly the performance of classifiers.

Keywords: Human activity recognition · Smart homes · Embedding · Word encoding · Fully Convolutional Network · Automatic features

1 Introduction

Human Activity Recognition (HAR) has been the focus of research efforts due to its key role for different ambient assisted living (AAL) domains as well as

The work is partially supported by project VITAAL and is financed by Brest Metropole, the region of Brittany and the European Regional Development Fund (ERDF).

© Springer Nature Singapore Pte Ltd. 2021
X. Li et al. (Eds.): DL-HAR 2020, CCIS 1370, pp. 111–125, 2021.
https://doi.org/10.1007/978-981-16-0575-8_9

the increasing demand for home automation and convenience services in daily activities. The main task of HAR is to recognize human activities from the data collected through environmental sensors and Internet of Things (IoT) devices. They use different sensor technologies such as cameras, wearable or low-level smart sensors to track human activities, as described in [6].

Recent advances in IoT technologies and the reduction of the cost of sensors are leading to the proliferation of these ambient devices and the development of smart homes. This is why in this work we will focus more on IoT-based HAR, as opposed to video or wearable-based HAR.

Along the development of the hardware, the HAR algorithms also need to solve the challenges of HAR in smart homes. Indeed, the number, the type but also the placement of sensors can significantly influence the performance of HAR systems. A system suitable for a given home may be completely inadequate in some other, due to different house configuration or user habits. The algorithms thus need to be robust to the variability of environments. Besides, while video-based HAR can leverage rich and redundant information from images and video streams, IoT based HAR faces the challenges of sparse and incomplete information and redundant models. In contrast to videos where objects and people appear on several pixels and over several video frames, the IoT network only detects changes in the environment that are within their range of detection and in their field of view, and is oblivious to most changes in the environment, which occur outside these ranges. When a change is captured, this detection often translates into a signal with a single value from one sensor. This sparsity entails the redundancy challenge: a set of signals from the same set of sensors can be caused by different activities. Thus, algorithms for HAR in smart homes need to address the challenges of variability, sparsity and redundancy.

To adapt to variations of environments and uses, algorithms for HAR have turned to machine learning methods, and more specifically Deep Learning (DL) algorithms. To deal with sparsity and redundancy, first, algorithms that can learn long-term dependencies have been developed so as to understand the context of sensor signals. Second, studies have also tried to introduce domain knowledge and contextualization of sensors signals, through a good feature representation of sensor events. But handcrafted features need a lot of pre-processing and reduce its adaptability to various environments. Therefore HAR algorithms need to automatically extract domain relevant representations.

In recent years, there have been significant improvements of DL techniques. They have been successfully applied to Natural Language Processing (NLP) and Time Series Classification (TSC). Respectively for automatic extraction of good feature representations through word embedding techniques and classifiers.

Our contributions are the following: 1) We apply for the first time the Fully Convolutional Networks (FCN) classifier from TSC on activity recognition in smart homes. 2) We propose to use frequency-based encoding with word embedding from NLP to improve automatic feature extraction. 3) We design an end to end framework to automatically extract key features and classify daily activities in smart homes by merging TSC classifier and NLP words encoding. 4)

Finally, we show that domain knowledge gained by event encoding and embedding improves significantly the performance of classifiers.

We propose in the following section to review the state-of-the-art HAR smart home classifiers, a TSC classifier and the existing feature representation methods, in particular those used in NLP applications. In Sect. 3, we will propose a framework combining a TSC algorithm and a NLP sequence features extractor method. In Sect. 5, we will report on the performance of our proposed framework before concluding.

2   Related Works

In this section, we describe the algorithms developed for HAR, and more generally for Time Serie Classification. We then examine how TSC can be bootstrapped by incorporating domain knowledge in feature encoding as in Natural Language Processing.

2.1   Traditional HAR Approaches

To recognize human activities based on sensor traces, researchers used various machine learning algorithms as reviewed in [15]. These can be divided into two streams: the algorithms exploiting a spatiotemporal representation, with Naive Bayes, Dynamic Bayesian Networks, Hidden Markov Models; and the algorithms based on features classification, with Decision Tree, Support Vector Machines, or Conditional Random Fields.

Most of these traditional HAR approaches commonly use handcrafted feature extraction methods. Automatic feature extraction is one of the challenges addressed by DL.

2.2   Deep Learning Approaches

Recently, a variety of DL algorithms have been applied for HAR to overcome those limitations and improve the performance of HAR. DL methods learn the features directly from the raw data hierarchically, to uncover high-level features. Long Short Term Memory (LSTM) can be seen as a very successful extension of the Recurrent Neural Networks (RNN), explicitly designed to deal with long-term dependencies. LSTMs allow automatic learning of temporal information from the sensor data without the need of handcrafted features or kernel fusion approaches, and have led to good performance in HAR in smart homes, as reported in [10,17]. [10] evaluated different LSTMs structures for HAR in smart homes. They show that the LSTM approach outperforms traditional HAR approaches in terms of classification score without using handcrafted features. LSTMs leads to a viable solution to significantly improve the HAR task in the smart home but suffers from training time.

Another DL approach, focusing more on pattern detection is Convolutional Neural Networks (CNNs). They have three advantages for HAR. They can capture local dependencies, that is, the importance of neighboring observations correlated with the current event. They are scale invariant in terms of step difference or event frequencies. In addition, they are able to learn a hierarchical representation of data. Researchers used 2D [4,13] and 1D [16] CNNs on HAR in smart homes. The 2D CNN obtained good classification results. But this approach is not robust enough to deal with unbalanced datasets, unlabeled events, and is not suitable for online recognition. 1D CNNs are competitive with LSTMs on sequence problems [16]. In general LSTMs obtain better performances due to their capacity to use long-term dependencies. But CNNs are faster to train and get accuracy levels close to LSTMs.

The FCN is a particular CNN, with only convolutional layers and no dense layers. FCN has shown compelling quality and efficiency for semantic segmentation of images [12]. Due to its performance on feature extraction, researchers transferred the FCN on TSC problems [19]. [3] compared the FCN against other TSC algorithms and obtained high classification performances. FCNs ranked first on 18 datasets out of 97 and in the top five on the others. However, no application of FCN for HAR in smart homes has been reported. For this reason we propose to apply the FCN to HAR in smart homes as a high-level extractor of features and classifier.

2.3   NLP and TSC Coupling

Works such as [18,20] have shown the importance of a good feature representation, but designing features for HAR applications is a tedious task.

DL algorithms can automatically extract features, they have widely shown to improve feature representation with words pre-processing for text classification in NLP. Researchers have devised many language models and different encoding of words. They proposed encodings such as n-gram, term frequency, term frequency-inverse document frequency, bag-of-words. Recently, they use DL algorithms such as word2vec, GloVe ELMo and more recently Transformers, coupled with the aforementioned encoding to achieve meaning word encoding [8,9]. DL algorithms infer features from the current input and to a lesser extent from past inputs, these encodings incorporate more general domain knowledge from the whole corpus. Their strong capacity to generate features from raw data and model word sequences increases the performance of DL classifiers. We propose to transpose previously cited NLP techniques on smart homes HAR problems in order to automatically generate key features.

Thus, we introduce in this article a DL methodology for HAR in smart homes inspired by the NLP and the TSC. We propose to combine the term frequency encoding and embedding with FCN, respectively: incorporate domain knowledge of event encoding in the first level of extraction features; and realize a higher-level of extraction features and the activity classification. The choice of the FCN algorithm from TSC is led by the output of the NLP embedding, which transforms the sequence classification problem into a multivariate TSC problem. To our knowledge this is the first time that a study has used FCN in smart-home activity recognition, and has combined it with embedding techniques to perform an end-to-end system that automatically extracts key features and classifies activities in smart homes.

3 Methodology

We merge NLP encoding and FCN classifier from TSC to deal with smart homes HAR. This coupling allows generating automatic key features and classify activities.

The framework architecture of the proposed method is shown in Fig. 1. First raw data from sensors are encoded into a sequence of indexes (Sect. 3.2), then are split using a sliding window (Sect. 3.4). The sliding windows are then processed through an embedding to extract a first level of features, and finally classified by the FCN (Sect. 3.3).

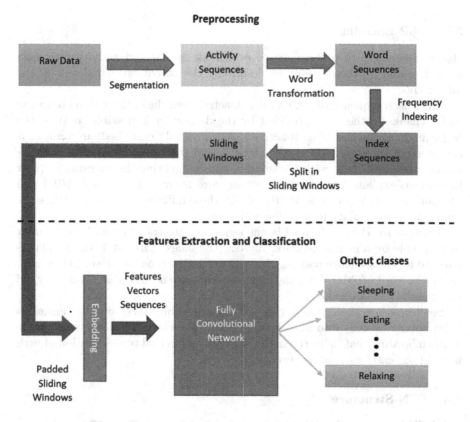

Fig. 1. Framework architecture of the proposed method

3.1   Problem Definition

The activity recognition problem is a classification problem. The goal is to attribute an activity label on sensors events sequences. We model our problem as follows. A set of sensors $S = \{s_1, ..., s_{|S|}\}$ produces events $e_i \in E$. An event is the value or the state returned by a sensor when the sensors emit a signal: $e_i = (s_i, v_i, t_i)$, where s_i is the sensor id, v_i the value returned by the sensor and t_i the time when the sensor changes its state or value. A sequence L_i is a trace of activity. L_i is a list of events $Seq_i = (e_i, ..., e_n)$. Each L_i can be associated to an activity label $a_i \in A$, by semantic segmentation.

In this paper we did not take in consideration the timestamp t_i when an event occurs. We simply ignore the parameter t for our experiments. We want to be able to recognize an activity regardless of the time of the day. For example, the activity "Sleeping" appears in general during the night but this activity can appear at any time during the day. Some people can work during the day and sleep by night and vice versa some people can work during the night and sleep during the day.

3.2   NLP Encoding

Our hypothesis is to process sensor events like words and activity sequences as text sentences; these sentences describing the activities carried out by the inhabitants.

First, each sequence of activity is extracted from the dataset as sentences in NLP. Thanks to the label provided by the dataset, it is possible to know the beginning and the end of each activity. As previously described, an event e_i is composed of the sensor ID s_i, the value v_i and the timestamp t_i. By concatenating the sensor ID s_i with his value v_i and by ignoring the timestamp t_i, for the reasons explained previously, a sensor word is created, e.g., $s_i = M001$ and the value $v_i = ON$ becomes $M001ON$. All these different text words define the smart home vocabulary to describe activities.

Then, as in NLP, each word in the sequences are transformed into an index to be usable by a neural network. In NLP the index starts at 1, the 0 value is reserved for the sequence padding. Indexes are assigned based on word frequency, e.g., if the word $M001ON$ has the highest occurrence in the dataset, the assigned index is the lowest one i.e. 1.

Sequences are then passed through an embedding layer which transforms index tokens (words) into auto learned features vectors. This creates a simple word embedding that helps the network to get an internal representation of each word in our cases each sensor event.

3.3   FCN Structure

The FCN is a particular CNN. Its structure only contains convolutional layers e.g., no fully connected layers for the classification part. The same structure as [3,19] is used in this paper.

This structure (Fig. 2) is composed of three blocks described by Eq. 1. Where x is the input, W the weight matrix, b the bias and $\otimes$ the convolution operator and h the hidden representation. Each block consists of a 1D convolutional layer with Batch Normalization (BN) [7] and a rectified linear unit (ReLU) activation to speed up the convergence and help improve generalizations.

$$y = W \otimes x + b$$
$$z = BN(y) \tag{1}$$
$$h = ReLU(z)$$

After the three convolution blocks, features are fed into a Global Average Pooling (GAP) layer [11]. GAP is a pooling operation designed to replace fully connected layers in classical CNNs. The idea is to generate one feature map for each corresponding category of the classification task. The resulting vector is fed directly into the softmax layer to realize the final classification.

One advantage of GAP over the fully connected layers is that it is more native to the convolution structure by enforcing correspondences between feature maps and categories. Thus, the feature maps can be easily interpreted as category confidence maps. Another advantage is that there is no parameter to optimize in the GAP thus over fitting is avoided at this layer. Furthermore, GAP sums out the spatial information; thus it is more robust to spatial translations of the input.

One of the advantages of FCNs is the invariance in the number of parameters across time series of different lengths. This invariance due to using a GAP layer enables the use of a transfer learning approach where one can train a model on a certain source dataset and fine-tune it on the target dataset [2].

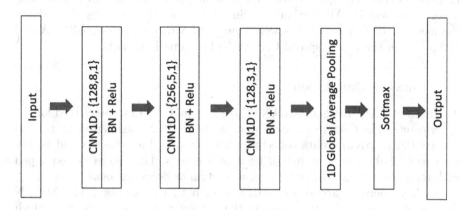

Fig. 2. Fully Convolutional Network (FCN) model core

3.4   Sliding Window

Contrary to LSTMs, CNNs must have a fixed input size and activity sequences can have different lengths, between 1 and more than 5000 events. To tackle this issue, a sliding window is applied over sequences. Using a sliding window also allows anticipating an online HAR. To fill windows with fewer events than the window size, a zero padding is used. The zero padding can impact the final result. To avoid too much zero in the sliding windows, a fine-tuned window size must be found.

For experiments, the Sensor Event Windows (SEW) [14] was used. The SEW approach divides the data into equal sensor event intervals. The size of a SEW is defined by a number of events. Therefore, the duration of the windows may vary. Authors of [14] compared different windows types and conclude that Time Windows (TW) provides the best accuracy and F-Measure score. They consider SEW as the second-best window method because SEW are able to classify more activities than TW. We assume this is because SEWs keep a fixed context size while it is variable for TWs. A stable context size allows the neural network to keep the same amount of information regardless of the window.

In this work, SEWs were used for two reasons. First, we want to evaluate the method for its ability to learn automatic features from the window context. The intuition being to train a network onto bounded activity sequences to extract features and then use them on streaming sensor data for online recognition. Second, this avoids too many zeros inside windows by controlling the number of events.

4   Experimental Setup

LSTMs provide very good results on sequence problems and go beyond traditional advanced HAR methods in Smart Homes [10]. In order to evaluate the method, LSTMs and FCNs were compared with two dataset ARUBA and MILAN from the widely spread CASAS [1] benchmark datasets.

4.1   Datasets Description

Two datasets, ARUBA and MILAN (Table 1) from CASAS were selected for the experiments. The CASAS datasets were introduced by Washington State University. Daily activities data collected, comes from real apartments and houses with real inhabitants, who live in their own houses. The houses are equipped with temperature and binary sensors, as motion or doors sensors.

A single person carried out activities in both the datasets. The MILAN dataset was selected for the noise on the dataset produced by the pet, which increases the difficulty of classification. They contain several months of labeled activities and are unbalanced, i.e., some activities are less represented than others. In addition these two datasets contain common and different activities with approximately the same number of sensors.

An unbalanced dataset increases the classification challenge. Indeed if some classes are less represented the system gets fewer examples to find the discriminating features. Moreover some events are unlabeled or unidentified and are tagged under the class name "Other". This class appears between 45% and 50% into these datasets. In the literature most researchers remove the class "Other" and balance the dataset by reducing the number of examples for each class.

This method creates a drawback, by ignoring unlabeled events it becomes a fixed classification problem. The system cannot make the difference between a known and an unknown class. This does not allow the system to be able to discover new sequences of activities.

Here the original distribution was kept. The objective was to evaluate the robustness of the method and the models.

Table 1. Details of datasets.

	Aruba	Milan
Habitants	1	1 + pet
Number of sensors	39	33
Number of activities	12	16
Number of days	219	82
Average sequence length	133	87.3

4.2 SEW Parameters

As previously described, sequences of activities were segmented in SEWs. Different SEWs sizes, 100, 75, 50, 25, with a stride of one was studied. This stride size allows the HAR process each time a new event is triggered. The goal is to find the best SEW size e.g., the minimal SEW size with the maximal information that allows to discriminate activities sequences with a high F1-score and high-balanced accuracy. The smaller the size of SEW, the faster an activity can be recognized in the case of online HAR.

4.3 Networks Parameters

FCNs parameters are the same as [3]. All convolutions have a stride equal to one with a zero padding to preserve the exact length of the time series after the convolution. The first convolution contains 128 filters and a length equal to 8, followed by a second convolution of 256 filters with a length equal to 5, which in turn is fed to a third and final convolutional layer composed of 128 filters, with a length equal to 3.

LSTMs parameters are the same as [10]. The LSTM cell is composed of 64 neurons and then followed by a softmax layer for the final classification.

As it is usually made in NLP an embedding layer was added between the raw data and the neural network. The number of neurons was fixed to 64 as it was defined in [10].

4.4 Hardware and Software Setup

Experiments were made on a server, with an Intel(R) Xeon(R) CPU E5-2640 v3 2.60 GHz, with 32 CPUs, 128 Go of RAM and a NVIDIA Tesla K80 graphic card. Keras and Tensorflow frameworks were used for the algorithm's implementation. The source code can be found at https://github.com/dbouchabou/Fully-Convolutional-Network-Smart-Homes.

4.5 Evaluation Method

To evaluate the proposed method, datasets were split into two parts: 70% for the train and 30% for the test. These two parts contain a shuffled stratified (over class) number of SEW of each activity. e.g., if the dataset contains 100 windows labeled "Sleeping" after shuffling, the 100 windows are split into two parts: 70 windows for the train set, 30 windows for the test set. The random shuffle helps the algorithm to get a better generalization and representation. The stratified forces both subsets to contain representations of each class.

A stratified (over class) threefold cross-validation procedure is performed on the training set. These three trains and three validation subsets are then used to train and validate algorithms.

During the training phase on each train set, early stop and best model selection methods proposed by the Tensorflow framework was used. These methods stop the training before overfitting and saves the best model of each train. The early stop condition is based on the validation loss value. If the current loss doesn't decrease after n epochs since the last, best model selected (here $n = 20$) the training is interrupted.

The three best trained models (one for each training subset) were evaluated on the test set to calculate the average balanced accuracy and the average weighted F1-score, because datasets are unbalanced.

To accelerate the training time by epoch and because the number of SEW is big, a batch size of 1024 was used for all experiments. No differences were noticed between the batch size evaluation during the tests, the results were similar except in training time.

5 Experimental Results

5.1 FCNs and LSTMs Performances

Table 2 and Table 3 show the performances of two FCNs and two LSTMs on raw sensor data for the two datasets. Vanilla LSTM, FCN and LSTM, FCN with an embedding layer on different windows size were evaluated. The average balanced accuracy and the average weighted F1-score was computed. FCN appears to obtain the best weighted F1-score with and without the embedding onto both datasets. The LSTM is close to or equal to the FCN on a large SEW, greater than 50. Compared to the FCN the LSTM looks to need more events to realize the classification.

From the balanced accuracy point of view, FCNs get best values except on the MILAN dataset when the window size is higher than 50. This decrease in performance is due to the zero padding. Indeed the average sequence length on the MILAN dataset is around 88 events. When the window size is close to or over this average, the performances of the FCN decrease. Some small sequences like "Bed to Toilet" or "Eve Meds" are not classified. This results in a drop in the balanced accuracy score.

As an online HAR is expected in our future work, it is interesting to observe the performance of the method on the small SEW size. The goal is to achieve

Table 2. Weighted F1 score and balanced accuracy in Aruba's dataset

Model	100	75	50	25
	Weighted avg F1 score (%)			
LSTM	96.67	94.67	90.67	85.00
FCN	99.00	98.00	97.67	92.33
LSTM + Embedding	**100.00**	99.67	98.00	90.00
FCN + Embedding	**100.00**	**100.00**	**100.00**	**99.00**
	Balanced accuracy (%)			
LSTM	81.45	76.09	71.05	83.30
FCN	88.85	87.41	87.08	80.32
LSTM + Embedding	94.55	93.61	90.20	74.81
FCN + Embedding	**95.37**	**95.07**	**94.89**	**92.44**

Table 3. Weighted F1 score and balanced accuracy in Milan's dataset

Model	100	75	50	25
	Weighted avg F1 score (%)			
LSTM	84.00	85.67	75.33	64.00
FCN	77.33	93.67	88.33	83.67
LSTM + Embedding	98.00	97.00	93.00	73.67
FCN + Embedding	**99.00**	**98.00**	**97.00**	**94.33**
	Balanced accuracy (%)			
LSTM	62.15	64.95	55.70	43.29
FCN	42.24	76.41	71.82	71.34
LSTM + Embedding	**88.52**	**86.77**	82.05	59.35
FCN + Embedding	84.23	86.64	**87.83**	**90.86**

HAR in as little time as possible, with as few events as possible, to get the most responsive system possible. In this case, the FCN obtained the best values with SEWs of sizes 50 and 25. Performances decrease as the SEW size decreases, but the FCN maintained a high score for balanced accuracy and the F1-score. Performance drops less with FCNs than with LSTMs. It seems that FCNs can generate more relevant automatic features than LSTMs on small sequences, therefore with less information.

5.2   Training Time

Table 4 and Table 5 show the average training time and the average amount of training epochs by SEWs size. On both datasets FCNs realized the shortest time on every SEWs size. The embedding layer allows to reduce the number of epochs and the total training time in the majority of cases. The training time

Table 4. Training time performance and number of epochs training in Aruba's dataset

Model	100	75	50	25
	Average epoch number			
LSTM	242	278	335	256
FCN	77	71	111	108
LSTM + Embedding	161	191	210	161
FCN + Embedding	67	62	71	98
	Average training time (HH:MM:SS)			
LSTM	06:28:42	06:43:08	06:29:58	03:00:26
FCN	00:58:00	00:52:15	01:20:35	00:51:27
LSTM + Embedding	04:45:56	04:45:38	04:14:35	02:02:53
FCN + Embedding	01:12:37	00:59:42	00:57:27	00:52:15

Table 5. Training time performance and number of epochs training in Milan's dataset

Model	100	75	50	25
	Average epoch number			
LSTM	274	385	365	324
FCN	45	101	87	145
LSTM + Embedding	255	290	320	183
FCN + Embedding	65	51	52	55
	Average training time (HH:MM:SS)			
LSTM	02:03:43	02:11:07	01:44:06	01:00:10
FCN	00:09:39	00:20:17	00:15:08	00:16:50
LSTM + Embedding	01:57:52	01:49:35	01:36:56	00:35:26
FCN + Embedding	00:16:24	00:11:42	00:10:00	00:07:67

is divided by 2 to 6 with the FCN depending on the window size compared to LSTM. This time saving is explained by the ease of parallelization of calculations of convolutional networks.

5.3   Encoding Impact

Tables 2, 3, 4 and 5 show that the embedding layer improves network performances. Indeed, with the embedding layer networks gain significant performance, 10% points on balanced accuracy in average. Sensor events are transformed into vectors of 64 automatically learned features that allow networks to maintain a high score on small SEWs.

During our experiments, we noticed that the frequency encoding strategy improved performance, unlike random or arbitrary index allocation. We think this ordering helps networks generate discriminators on important events or rare events.

6   Conclusion

We have proposed a new method that coupled for the first time FCNs and embedding based on frequency encoding for HAR in smart homes. Our assessment on two datasets shows that:

- The embedding based on frequency encoding significantly improves the performance of LSTM and FCN in all cases. This means that the domain knowledge incorporated in the embedding can improve the understanding of events by LSTM and FCN.
- With the same encoding, FCNs obtain the same or better performance than LSTMs, with the exception of only two configurations and are quicker to train.
- Moreover, FCNs outperform LSTMs when the window size decreases. This means that FCNs have a shorter delay in recognizing activities, and are more suitable for real-time activity recognition.

The proposed framework is pure end-to-end without any heavy pre-processing on the raw data or feature crafting, thanks to frequency-based encoding and the embedding. This method appears to be relevant for HAR problems in smart homes with low-level sensors.

7   Discussion and Future Directions

The results presented in this paper show that the applied DL approach based on NLP encoding and FCN is a relevant solution to significantly improve the smart homes HAR task.

We used a naive embedding based on frequency encoding that improved classification results. We plan to explore more word embedding techniques [9] such as Word2Vec or ELMo to improve the latent knowledge space and in the process enhance classification performances. Indeed these techniques take into account the context of words.

In addition, we are only experimenting with offline HAR. But the usage of SEWs in our assessment showed relevant results so we want to apply this to online HAR applications.

Moreover we plan to evaluate other windowing methods as TW or Fuzzy Windows [5] with this method. To study which window methods produce the fastest and most accurate online HAR in smart homes.

References

1. Cook, D.J., Crandall, A.S., Thomas, B.L., Krishnan, N.C.: CASAS: a smart home in a box. Computer **46**(7), 62–69 (2012)
2. Fawaz, H.I., Forestier, G., Weber, J., Idoumghar, L., Muller, P.A.: Transfer learning for time series classification. In: 2018 IEEE International Conference on Big Data (Big Data), pp. 1367–1376. IEEE (2018)
3. Ismail Fawaz, H., Forestier, G., Weber, J., Idoumghar, L., Muller, P.-A.: Deep learning for time series classification: a review. Data Min. Knowl. Discov. **33**(4), 917–963 (2019). https://doi.org/10.1007/s10618-019-00619-1
4. Gochoo, M., Tan, T.H., Liu, S.H., Jean, F.R., Alnajjar, F.S., Huang, S.C.: Unobtrusive activity recognition of elderly people living alone using anonymous binary sensors and DCNN. IEEE J. Biomed. Health Inform. **23**(2), 693–702 (2018)
5. Hamad, R.A., Hidalgo, A.S., Bouguelia, M.R., Estevez, M.E., Quero, J.M.: Efficient activity recognition in smart homes using delayed fuzzy temporal windows on binary sensors. IEEE J. Biomed. Health Inform. **24**(2), 387–395 (2019)
6. Hussain, Z., Sheng, M., Zhang, W.E.: Different approaches for human activity recognition: a survey. arXiv preprint arXiv:1906.05074 (2019)
7. Ioffe, S., Szegedy, C.: Batch normalization: accelerating deep network training by reducing internal covariate shift. arXiv preprint arXiv:1502.03167 (2015)
8. Kowsari, K., Jafari Meimandi, K., Heidarysafa, M., Mendu, S., Barnes, L., Brown, D.: Text classification algorithms: a survey. Information **10**(4), 150 (2019)
9. Li, Q., et al.: A survey on text classification: from shallow to deep learning. arXiv e-prints. arXiv-2008 (2020)
10. Liciotti, D., Bernardini, M., Romeo, L., Frontoni, E.: A sequential deep learning application for recognising human activities in smart homes. Neurocomputing **396**, 501–513 (2019). https://doi.org/10.1016/j.neucom.2018.10.104
11. Lin, M., Chen, Q., Yan, S.: Network in network. arXiv preprint arXiv:1312.4400 (2013)
12. Long, J., Shelhamer, E., Darrell, T.: Fully convolutional networks for semantic segmentation. In: Proceedings of the IEEE Conference on Computer Vision and Pattern Recognition, pp. 3431–3440 (2015)
13. Mohmed, G., Lotfi, A., Pourabdollah, A.: Employing a deep convolutional neural network for human activity recognition based on binary ambient sensor data. In: Proceedings of the 13th ACM International Conference on PErvasive Technologies Related to Assistive Environments, pp. 1–7 (2020)
14. Quigley, B., Donnelly, M., Moore, G., Galway, L.: A comparative analysis of windowing approaches in dense sensing environments. In: Proceedings, vol. 2, no. 19, p. 1245 (October 2018). https://doi.org/10.3390/proceedings2191245. http://dx.doi.org/10.3390/proceedings2191245

15. Sedky, M., Howard, C., Alshammari, T., Alshammari, N.: Evaluating machine learning techniques for activity classification in smart home environments. Int. J. Inf. Syst. Comput. Sci. **12**(2), 48–54 (2018)
16. Singh, D., Merdivan, E., Hanke, S., Kropf, J., Geist, M., Holzinger, A.: Convolutional and recurrent neural networks for activity recognition in smart environment. In: Holzinger, A., Goebel, R., Ferri, M., Palade, V. (eds.) Towards Integrative Machine Learning and Knowledge Extraction. LNCS (LNAI), vol. 10344, pp. 194–205. Springer, Cham (2017). https://doi.org/10.1007/978-3-319-69775-8_12
17. Singh, D., et al.: Human activity recognition using recurrent neural networks. In: Holzinger, A., Kieseberg, P., Tjoa, A.M., Weippl, E. (eds.) CD-MAKE 2017. LNCS, vol. 10410, pp. 267–274. Springer, Cham (2017). https://doi.org/10.1007/978-3-319-66808-6_18
18. Tahir, S.F., Fahad, L.G., Kifayat, K.: Key feature identification for recognition of activities performed by a smart-home resident. J. Ambient Intell. Humaniz. Comput. **11**(5), 2105–2115 (2019). https://doi.org/10.1007/s12652-019-01236-y
19. Wang, Z., Yan, W., Oates, T.: Time series classification from scratch with deep neural networks: a strong baseline. In: 2017 International Joint Conference on Neural Networks (IJCNN), pp. 1578–1585. IEEE (2017)
20. Yan, S., Lin, K.J., Zheng, X., Zhang, W.: Using latent knowledge to improve real-time activity recognition for smart IoT. IEEE Trans. Knowl. Data Eng. **32**, 574–587 (2019)

Towards User Friendly Medication Mapping Using Entity-Boosted Two-Tower Neural Network

Shaoqing Yuan[1]([⊠]) [iD], Parminder Bhatia[2], Busra Celikkaya[2] [iD], Haiyang Liu[1], and Kyunghwan Choi[1]

[1] Amazon Alexa, Seattle, WA 98121, USA
{shaoqiny,lhaiyang,kyunghwa}@amazon.com
[2] Amazon AWS, Seattle, WA 98121, USA
{parmib,busrac}@amazon.com

Abstract. Recent advancements in medical entity linking have been applied in the area of scientific literature and social media data. However, with the adoption of telemedicine and conversational agents such as Alexa in healthcare settings, medical name inference has become an important task. Medication name inference is the task of mapping user friendly medication names from a free-form text to a concept in a normalized medication list. This is challenging due to the differences in the use of medical terminology from health care professionals and user conversations coming from the lay public. We begin with mapping descriptive medication phrases (DMP) to standard medication names (SMN). Given the prescriptions of each patient, we want to provide them with the flexibility of referring to the medication in their preferred ways. We approach this as a ranking problem which maps SMN to DMP by ordering the list of medications in the patient's prescription list obtained from pharmacies. Furthermore, we leveraged the output of intermediate layers and performed medication clustering. We present the Medication Inference Model (MIM) achieving state-of-the-art results. By incorporating medical entities based attention, we have obtained further improvement for ranking models.

Keywords: Text matching · NLP · Medication name

1 Introduction

Medication names are extremely hard to pronounce for patients without a proper medical background. Thus, when interacting with Alexa on medication names, patients without this background may have many different ways to refer to a medication (e.g., Bumetanide can be referred to as Bumetanide (generic name), Bumex (brand name), high blood pressure pill (disease name)). On the other hand, patients with medical knowledge may use abbreviations or specialized ways to refer to medication names. For example, patients may use "immune

X. Li et al. (Eds.): DL-HAR 2020, CCIS 1370, pp. 126–138, 2021.
https://doi.org/10.1007/978-981-16-0575-8_10

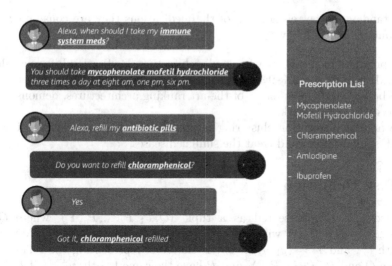

Fig. 1. Different ways of how users interact with conversational agents for medical queries

meds" to refer to "mycophenolate mofetil hydrochloride" in their prescription list (Fig. 1).

In this paper, we describe a new problem about finding the generic medication name (SMN: standardized medication name) based on a patient's description (DMP: descriptive medication phrase) from a list of medications the patient is consuming. According to our internal user research, in the United States, patients with chronic diseases usually take around four to five medications daily. This problem is different from medical concept normalization [1] which tries to map a health-related entity mention in a free-form text to a concept in a controlled vocabulary [2] which is a generic concept list rather than a patient specific prescription list and is generally much longer.

We structure this as a ranking problem. Here we rank all medications a patient is consuming based on the relationship with the patient's description and the one ranked highest will be the inference result. We present a hard attention based entity boosted CNN architecture achieving 4% over earlier ranking methods.

Furthermore, the mapping between SMN and DMP contains the patient's understanding of the medications, especially from the usage perspective of the medications. Using latent output from our model, we build a medication clustering system which groups together medications with similar effects and disease treatments. The output is designed to aid physicians to consider other medications as a substitution for decreasing cost as well as helping patients distinguish medications that are similar in their impression but should, in reality, be used in different conditions. Moreover, with clustering patients will have an intuitive understanding of the relationship of the medications they are consuming. Our contributions are as follows:

- We present a medical entity boosted architecture, Medication Inference Model (MIM) achieving a 7%–9% improvement over strong BERT baselines.
- We benchmark against state-of-the-art ranking architectures, demonstrating robustness of our work.
- We present medication clustering results which group together medications with similar effects and treat the similar diseases.

2   Task Definition

Each example is represented as a tuple $(Q, P_1, P_2, ..., P_n, Y)$, where $Q = (q_1, q_2, ..., q_{l_q})$ is a DMP, with a length l_q, $P_i = (p_1, p_2, ...p_{l_{p_i}})$ is a SMN, with a length l_{p_i}, and $Y = (y_1, y_2, ..., y_n)$ is the label representing the relationship between Q and $P_1, P_2, ..., P_n$. Y and P have the same length. $y_i = 1$ if P_i is the generic medication name that Q is referring to, 0 otherwise.

Y	$Q = \{q_1(\text{high}), q_2(\text{blood}), q_3(\text{pressure})\}$
$y_1 = 0$	$P_1 = \{p_1(\text{morphine}), p_2(\text{suppository})\}$
$y_2 = 1$	$P_2 = \{p_1(\text{hydrochlorothiazide})\}$
$y_3 = 0$	$P_3 = \{...\}$
...	...

It is possible that among $P_1, P_2, ..., P_n$, more than one medications may be referred to by Q. Thus, $\sum_{i=0}^{n} y_i = m$ where m is the number of medications in $P_1, P_2, ..., P_n$ that could be referred by Q. Ideally, we should make it possible that for the estimated $\hat{Y}$, $\sum_{i=0}^{n} \hat{y}_i > 1$. In this paper, however, we assume $\sum_{i=0}^{n} y_i = 1$.

The clustering task is defined as grouping medications across the prescriptions of different patients. i.e., we assign each medication in $(P_1, P_2, ..., P_N)$ to a group according to the DMP Q associated with them.

3   Method

Instead of comparing n medications in each sample, we begin with two. Each sample consists of (Q, P_1, P_2, Y) and the model must distinguish which SMN in P_1, P_2 the patient is referring to by Q. To simplify, we assume only one of (P_1, P_2) could be referred by Q. In practice, when there are n (where $n > 2$) medications in a patient's prescription we run the model on all the combinations of the medications and rank them accordingly.

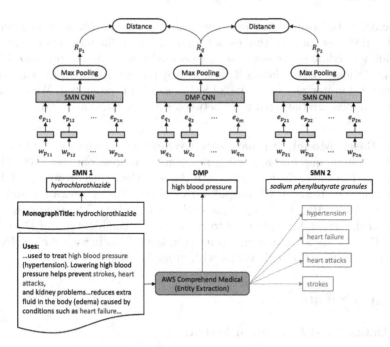

Fig. 2. Medication inference model structure

3.1 Entity Boosted Two-Tower Neural Network

Motivated by the facial recognition problem, where the models evaluate the similarity between images of faces [3], we apply a Two-tower neural network to our problem. We regard the DMP as the query of each medicine and the SMNs as the medication candidates. The purpose is to match the correct SMNs to the DMP provided.

Descriptions can often be verbose and can contain a large amount of noise. To improve the robustness and reduce noise, we have incorporated medical entity based hard attention [4] using Amazon Web Services Comprehend Medical (CM) [5] which is a natural language processing service to perform entity and relation extraction.

For each instance of data, we use the generic name as the SMN in our model, and generate DMPs from free-form text data that describe the usage of each medication in patient friendly terms. To reduce the noise, we feed the description to CM to extract entities. CM is able to extract relevant medical information from unstructured text and classify extracted entities into five categories and 28 types. In this work we use the entities marked with types "dx name" (diagnostic indicator), "treatment name", "system organ site", "swap", "generic name", "procedure name", "brand name", "test name" as DMPs.

Medication Inference Model. Figure 2 outlines the Medication Inference Model (MIM) network. In this model, there are two different sets of unshared embedding weights, where one is used to embed SMNs and the other DMP. We use convolutional (CNN) layers [6] followed by pooling on top of the embedding layer to get a vector representation of SMNs and DNP separately. We use cosine distance to measure the separation between the two SMNs and DMP.

BERT-Based Model. It is natural to leverage models which prove to be successful in solving question-answering problems to process our task. Here, DMP are regarded as the patient's query, with the n SMNs as the answer candidates.

We concatenate the DMP output with different SMNs separately and combine them into a BERT [7] based multi-choice model [8]. The vector representations of the [CLS] tokens are used to represent the combinations of DMP with each SMN, and are fed into a fully connected layer. Finally we use hinge loss for ranking to compare the scale values with ground truth.

4   Experiments

4.1   Dataset and Evaluation Metrics

Synthetic Data Set. The training and test dataset are generated from 2,683 medication descriptions from the FDB[1] PEM (patient education module) dataset. FDB stands for First DataBank which is a known drug database and medical device database provider. Each PEM file contains a patient facing medication description including medication generic name, uses, warnings side effects etc.[2]

The SMNs are collected from the generic name section and DMPs are generated from the "USES" section of the PEM files using CM as described in Sect. 3.1. To evaluate the effect of the entity extraction component, we generate another DMP set by randomly drawing n-grams (where $n = [1, 2, 3, 4, 5]$) from the "USES" section of the PEM files as a replacement for CM.

Next, we use the SMNs and DMPs collected to generate our training and test sets. We generate each instance starting with a DMP according to following steps.

1. For each DMP, we generate a positive SMNs set which consist of SMNs extracted from the same PEM file where the DMP is extracted from. It is possible that one DMP may have multiple positive SMNs if the DMP is a very general phrase. For example, the DMP "high blood pressure" may have multiple SMNs since many medications can be used to treat hypertension.

---

[1] https://www.fdbhealth.com/.

[2] CommonNames, Warning, Uses, HowToUse, SideEffects, Precautions, DrugInteractions, Overdose, Notes, MissedDose, Storage, MedicAlert.

2. For each DMP, we also generate a negative SMN set. The negative SMNs are all the medications covered by the PEM files excluding the positive SMNs identified above and should follow the constraint that the entities extracted from the "USES" section of the negative SMNs' PEM files should have no overlap with that of the DMPs.
3. Each instance in the training and validation data set consists of 1 positive SMN and $n - 1$ negative SMNs randomly selected from the SMN sets described above. The label of each instance is indicating which SMN is positive.

For the training and validation splits, n is set to 2 in step 3 above, which means there are two SMNs in each instance. The training and validation data set contains 680K instances and 70% of them are used for training and 30% for validation and testing.

For testing purposes, we generated four synthetic test sets with n in step 3 set to $2, 3, 4, 5$ separately to simulate the real situations where patients with chronic disease in the U.S. usually have four to five medications in their prescription list at a time.

Real Data Set. The real data set is generated based on 251 prescriptions collected from the i2b2 data set[3] which contains the de-identified patient discharge summaries. Internal human annotators generate DMPs for each medication in the prescriptions. It is observed that in a real prescription, multiple medications may serve the same purpose and a general DMP could be used to refer to multiple medications in a prescription. In our current experiment, we assume the ground truth of each DMP is only the medication used to generate the DMP in a prescription. In this way, we will get the lower bound of the performance of the models. For testing purpose, we limited the number of medications in each prescription to be 10, 5, 4, 3, 2 respectively. For the test set with 10 as max number of medications, we go through all the 251 prescriptions and only select the prescriptions that has less than 10 medications into our test set. We randomly truncate the prescriptions in the 10 medication test set to 5, 4, 3, 2 medications as the other test sets. Further more, in order to evaluate the situations where one DMP may refer to multiple SMNs in a prescription, the annotators are currently working on labeling all the SMNs that a DMP could refer to in a prescription and if the model outputs one of the medications in the ground truth SMNs, the test sample will be marked as success in future experiments.

We report accuracy as the main evaluation metric, i.e., the correctness of selecting the positive SMN from n SMNs. When evaluating on the test data, the model goes through all pairwise combinations of the SMNs and ranks all the SMNs accordingly.

4.2 Experimental Details

For the CNN-based model, we test multiple word embedding models including 200-dimensional BioWordVec [9,10] and 300-dimensional FastText word

---

[3] https://portal.dbmi.hms.harvard.edu/projects/n2c2-nlp/.

embeddings [11] trained with 3,466 articles from the Mayo Clinic. The two dimensional CNN layer consisted of 200 filters with window size 2, strip as 1 and no regularization. Batch size is set to 150 and we observed model convergence after six epochs. For the pre-trained language model, we leverage Clinical BERT [12], BioBERT [13], and original BERT models [7]. We used the default settings for all BERT models as provided by [7]. Batch size is set to 32, learning rate is set to 5×10^{-5} and dropout rate is set to 0.2. We observed the model converged after 10 epochs. We trained and evaluated all the models using a Tesla V100 GPU.

Baselines. When evaluating the performance of our model, we compare the medication name inference performance with baseline models listed below.

- **ARC-I** [14]: ARC-I finds the representation of each sentence with CNN layers, and then compares the representation for the two sentences with a multilayer perceptron (MLP).
- **ARC-II** [14]: ARC-II improves based on ARC-I by calculating the interaction features between sentences with CNN.
- **ConvKNRM** [15]: Conv-KNRM uses CNN to represent n-grams of various lengths and soft matches them in a unified embedding space. The n-gram soft matches are then utilized by the kernel pooling and a fully connected layer to generate the final ranking score.
- **MatchLSTM** [16]: The matchLSTM sequentially aggregates the matching of the attention-weighted question to each token of the answer and uses the aggregated matching result to make a final prediction.
- **MatchPyramid** [17]: MatchPyramid generates a matching matrix which represents the similarity between mention and candidate and then apply CNN layers on top of the matrix followed by a MLP layer to calculate the similarity score.

5   Results and Discussion

Table 1 provides the accuracy results for each model we experimented with on the synthetic test data set. Number of candidates represent test data sets with $2, 3, 4, 5$ medications in each test instance, as described in Sect. 4.1. We report test results for each model with and without AWS Comprehend Medical as "Entity-based Attention" and "Baseline" columns.

Table 1 demonstrates the robustness of MIM. We observe that MIM and BERT based models outperform current state-of-the-art models such as ARC-I and MatchPyramid across a different number of candidates. Table 2 further compares the performance of two best performing models on real test set.

MIM outperforms BERT based models with a 7–9% improvement in accuracy. We believe the major reason for this is that MIM, by encoding SMN and DMP separately, is able to encode the representation in a more robust way

Table 1. Synthetic test set: For each model we report top1 accuracy including and excluding entity-based attention.

Number of candidates								
Model	Baseline				Entity-based attention			
	2	3	4	5	2	3	4	5
NormalBert	69.7	54.7	46.6	42.7	79.7	72.7	62.4	62.5
BioBert	73.4	**59.8**	**51.9**	46.4	81.5	74.8	66.2	66.4
ClinicalBert	73.5	57.8	**51.9**	47.4	79.5	74.4	64.8	62.7
ARC-1	65.2	46.2	37.5	33.4	76.8	66.8	58.6	59.4
ARC-2	64.0	48.1	39.1	36.5	75.7	65.7	62.1	57.0
ConvKNRM	65.4	52.0	42.6	38.8	76.7	66.6	60.7	57.3
MatchLSTM	64.9	50.8	40.9	35.4	82.4	70.9	62.6	58.3
MatchPyramid	59.5	45.0	36.5	33.5	74.0	58.0	58.0	54.1
MIM	**73.9**	57.9	48.9	**49.7**	**87.7**	**80.8**	**78.9**	**76.9**

Table 2. Real test set: For each model we report top1 accuracy.

Upper limit for number of candidates				
Model	2	3	4	5	10
BioBert	83.10	73.50	67.00	61.8	52.70
MIM	**83.50**	**74.50**	**69.50**	**63.60**	**53.80**

in comparison to BERT based models which concatenate the representations together using a special separator token. We also observe performance variation of BERT models based on their pre-training. We found that domain specific pre-training helps, giving 2-3% improvement when compared to the baseline BERT.

We observe the entity-boosted description gives robust results across all the model settings achieving significant improvement in accuracy over non-entity based models. This alleviates the problem of noise in the lengthy descriptions.

Furthermore we see that our MIM model, with a relatively simpler CNN encoder as well as separate encoders for SMN and DMP, has the distinct advantage of generating inference results with low latency. This is ideal for real-time industrial settings. According to our experiments, the average latency for the MIM model for five medications is 10ms, while, compared against BERT at 89 ms.

5.1 Medication Clustering Result

We apply k-nearest neighbor (KNN) clustering based on the CNN max pooling output from the Two-tower neural network. The generic names of 2,683 medications are represented by vectors of 200 dimension. The number of clusters of KNN is determined by a Silhouette analysis [18] with result given in Fig. 3.

The Silhouette analysis shows that clustering performs better when number of classes is 31.

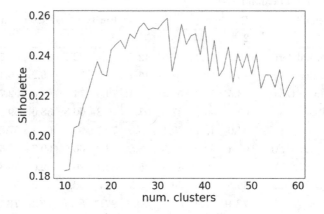

Fig. 3. Average Silhouette value for different number of clusters

Figure 4 shows the t-SNE visualization of the result where 2,683 medications are grouped into 31 clusters. The figure illustrates that medications with same effects, treating same disease or having similar drug types are mapped close to each other.

Table 3. Examples of the DMP/SMN match and clustering results

	(a) Diagnose	(b) Symptom	(c) Drug type
DMP	High blood pressure, strokes, heart attacks	Cough, coughing	Antibiotic
Example SMN	Amlodipine	Promethazine	Chloramphenicol
Nearby SMNs	Perindopril, ramipril, trandolapril, quinapril, enalapril, isradipine, lisinopril, sacubitril, aliskiren, eplerenone	Dextromethorphan, guaifenesin, expectorant, antihistamine, acetaminophen, hydrocodone, zanamivir	Polymyxin b, gentamicin, cefotetan, spiramycin, gatifloxacin, piperacillin, cephalexin, cefoxitin, ofloxacin

Table 3 shows three examples of the clustering result. The nearby SMNs are sampled from the same cluster which example SMNs belong to and ranked according to their distance to the given SMN. The nature of the problem enables and requires the inference model to group SMNs based on multiple dimensions. We list examples from three dimensions and it is very natural for users to refer to their medications by diagnosis, disease symptoms and drug type. For example, coughing is a common symptom for multiple diseases including the common cold, pulmonary diseases such as pneumonia, and even from seasonal allergies. In column (b), the model is able to cluster medications that could relieve cough

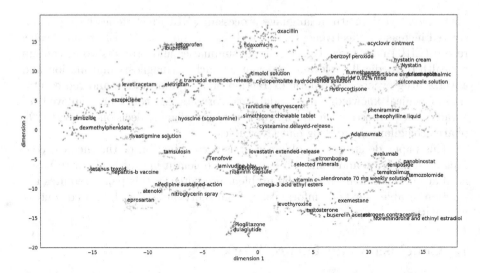

Fig. 4. t-SNE visualization of the clusters

symptom of different underlying causes, for example, promethazine and antihistamine are used to treat allergies whereas zanamivir is used to treat and prevent flu.

6   Related Work

Earlier work on medical concept normalization [1] relied on lexicon based string matching and dictionary lookup to map limited number of variations of text to a pre-defined medical vocabulary [19,20]. [21] introduced DNrom as the first pairwise learning ranking model that compares associations between mentions and entities of various disease. [22,23] then further leveraged deep learning models, convolutional neural network [22] and recurrent neural network models [24] trained on large corpus of medical articles etc. Currently, researchers enhanced the deep learning based model with different model structure to incorporate context information, better process out of vocabulary (OOV) words and take advantages of interaction features from different semantic levels [2,25,26].

With the success of deep learning, many neural network based models have been proposed for semantic matching, and document ranking. Models such as ARC-I [14] first compute the representation of the two sentences, and then compute their relevance. Semantic/text matching techniques fits well to solve the medical concept normalization problems when the number of candidates is limited. As listed in [8], recently researchers have focused on developing deep learning models to solve document retrieval, question answering, conversational response ranking, and paraphrase identification [8] problems and introduced state-of-the-art models such as ARC-I [14], ARC-II [14], ConvKNRM [15], MatchLSTM [16], MatchPyramid [17], Bert [7].

In recent years, natural language processing (NLP) techniques have demonstrated increasing effectiveness in clinical text mining [5,27] . Electronic health record (EHR) narratives, e.g., discharge summaries and progress notes contain a wealth of medically relevant information such as diagnosis information and adverse drug events. Automatic extraction of such information and representation of clinical knowledge in standardized formats [28] could be employed for a variety of purposes such as clinical event surveillance, decision support [29], pharmacovigilance, and drug efficacy studies.

This paper describes a problem that is a combination of the medical concept normalization and semantic matching problem using medical entity based hard attention. The nature of the problem presented in this paper requires the solution be able to extract informations from short phrases with limited context information.

7   Conclusion and Future Work

In this paper, we introduce a new problem common in the development of medication voice interaction products. We evaluate the accuracy of different solutions and show that our entity boosted MIM outperform baseline models. The specialty of this problem is that the context information is very limited when compared against other NLP tasks and the short length of the phrases prevent us from leveraging other advanced techniques that rely on words relationship in a phrase. The evaluation result also show that the problem prefers simple model structure. Since the phrases structure is very simple, the quality of word embeddings is more important in this problem and keeping the embedding weight unchanged is important when the training data is not sufficient enough to enhance the relationship between words either due to the nature of the data or small sample sizes.

We also observe the discrepancy between synthetic collected datasets from real patients. For example, the combinations of the medicine on synthetic prescriptions may not be valid from a practitioner's or patient's perspective. We plan to further validate our model on real patient data to increase practicality. Finally on top of comparing and evaluating on two medications samples, we plan to experiment with more medications in each sample in training to closer mimic real world scenarios.

References

1. Zhu, M., Celikkaya, B., Bhatia, P., Reddy, C.K.: LATTE: latent type modeling for biomedical entity linking. arXiv preprint arXiv:1911.09787 (2019)
2. Miftahutdinov, Z., Tutubalina, E.: Deep neural models for medical concept normalization in user-generated texts. arXiv preprint arXiv:1907.07972 (2019)
3. Chopra, S., Hadsell, R., LeCun, Y.: Learning a similarity metric discriminatively, with application to face verification. In: 2005 IEEE Computer Society Conference on Computer Vision and Pattern Recognition (CVPR'05), vol. 1, pp. 539–546. IEEE (2005)

4. Luong, M.-T., Pham, H., Manning, C.D.: Effective approaches to attention-based neural machine translation. arXiv preprint arXiv:1508.04025 (2015)
5. Bhatia, P., Celikkaya, B., Khalilia, M., Senthivel, S.: Comprehend medical: A named entity recognition and relationship extraction web service. In: 2019 18th IEEE International Conference On Machine Learning And Applications (ICMLA), pp. 1844–1851 (2019)
6. Kim, Y.: Convolutional neural networks for sentence classification. In: Proceedings of the 2014 Conference on Empirical Methods in Natural Language Processing (EMNLP), Doha, Qatar, October 2014, pp. 1746–1751. Association for Computational Linguistics (2014)
7. Devlin, J., Chang, M.-W., Lee, K., Toutanova, K.: BERT: pre-training of deep bidirectional transformers for language understanding. arXiv preprint arXiv:1810.04805 (2018)
8. Guo, J., Fan, Y., Ji, X., Cheng, X.: MatchZoo: a learning, practicing, and developing system for neural text matching. In: Proceedings of the 42Nd International ACM SIGIR Conference on Research and Development in Information Retrieval, SIGIR 2019, pp. 1297–1300. ACM, New York (2019)
9. Zhang, Y., Chen, Q., Yang, Z., Lin, H., Zhiyong, L.: BioWordVec, improving biomedical word embeddings with subword information and MeSH. Sci. Data **6**(1), 52 (2019)
10. Chen, Q., Peng, Y., Lu, Z.: BiosentVec: creating sentence embeddings for biomedical texts. CoRR, abs/1810.09302 (2018)
11. Bojanowski, P., Grave, E., Joulin, A., Mikolov, T.: Enriching word vectors with subword information. Trans. Assoc. Comput. Linguist. **5**, 135–146 (2017)
12. Alsentzer, E., et al.: Publicly available clinical BERT embeddings. In: Proceedings of the 2nd Clinical Natural Language Processing Workshop, Minneapolis, Minnesota, USA, pp. 72–78. Association for Computational Linguistics, June 2019
13. Lee, J., et al.: BioBERT: a pre-trained biomedical language representation model for biomedical text mining. Bioinformatics **36**, 1234–1240 (2019)
14. Hu, B., Lu, Z., Li, H., Chen, Q.: Convolutional neural network architectures for matching natural language sentences. In: Advances in Neural Information Processing Systems, pp. 2042–2050 (2014)
15. Dai, Z., Xiong, C., Callan, J., Liu, Z.: Convolutional neural networks for soft-matching n-grams in ad-hoc search. In: Proceedings of the Eleventh ACM International Conference on Web Search and Data Mining, pp. 126–134 (2018)
16. Wang, S., Jiang, J.: Machine comprehension using match-LSTM and answer pointer. arXiv preprint arXiv:1608.07905 (2016)
17. Pang, L., Lan, Y., Guo, J., Xu, J., Wan, S., Cheng, X.: Text matching as image recognition. In: Thirtieth AAAI Conference on Artificial Intelligence (2016)
18. Rousseeuw, P.J.: Silhouettes: a graphical aid to the interpretation and validation of cluster analysis. J. Comput. Appl. Math. **20**, 53–65 (1987)
19. Aronson, A.R.: Effective mapping of biomedical text to the UMLS metathesaurus: the metamap program. In: Proceedings of the AMIA Symposium, p. 17. American Medical Informatics Association (2001)
20. Brennan, P.F., Aronson, A.R.: Towards linking patients and clinical information: detecting UMLS concepts in e-mail. J. Biomed. Inf. **36**(4–5), 334–341 (2003)
21. Leaman, R., Doğan, R.I., Lu, Z.: DNorm: disease name normalization with pairwise learning to rank. Bioinformatics **29**(22), 2909–2917 (2013)
22. Limsopatham, N., Collier, N.: Normalising medical concepts in social media texts by learning semantic representation. Association for Computational Linguistics (2016)

23. Lee, K., Hasan, S.A., Farri, O., Choudhary, A., Agrawal, A.: Medical concept normalization for online user-generated texts. In: 2017 IEEE International Conference on Healthcare Informatics (ICHI), pp. 462–469. IEEE (2017)

24. Belousov, M., Dixon, W., Nenadic, G.: Using an ensemble of generalised linear and deep learning models in the SMM4H 2017 medical concept normalisation task. In: Proceedings of the Second Workshop on Social Media Mining for Health Applications (SMM4H). Health Language Processing Laboratory (2017)

25. Luo, Y., Song, G., Li, P., Qi, Z.: Multi-task medical concept normalization using multi-view convolutional neural network. In: Thirty-Second AAAI Conference on Artificial Intelligence (2018)

26. Niu, J., Yang, Y., Zhang, S., Sun, Z., Zhang, W.: Multi-task character-level attentional networks for medical concept normalization. Neural Process. Lett. **49**(3), 1239–1256 (2019)

27. Bhatia, P., Arumae, K., Busra Celikkaya, E.: Dynamic transfer learning for named entity recognition. In: Shaban-Nejad, A., Michalowski, M. (eds.) W3PHAI 2019. SCI, vol. 843, pp. 69–81. Springer, Cham (2020). https://doi.org/10.1007/978-3-030-24409-5_7

28. Singh, G., Bhatia, P.: Relation extraction using explicit context conditioning. arXiv preprint arXiv:1902.09271 (2019)

29. Jin, M., et al.: Improving hospital mortality prediction with medical named entities and multimodal learning. arXiv preprint arXiv:1811.12276 (2018)

Author Index

Printed in the United States
By Bookmasters